THE BRITISH ON BROADWAY

To Gerald and Colman

THE BRITISH ON BROADWAY

BACKSTAGE AND BEYOND—THE EARLY YEARS

Follow the Footsteps of the Legendary Knights,
Irving, Olivier and Coward

A Guide to the British Invasion of Broadway Including Walks through New York's Theatreland

by Elizabeth Sharland

To Francesca —

Best wishes

Elizabeth Sharland

BARBICAN PRESS

First published in 1999 by Barbican Press
c/o Amolibros, 5 Saxon Close, Watchet, Somerset TA23 0BN

Distributed by Gazelle Book Services Limited
Falcon House
Queen Square
Lancaster England LA1 1RN

British Library Cataloguing in Publication Data
A catalogue record for this book is available from the British Library

ISBN 0-9531930-1-2

This publication is managed by Amolibros, Watchet, Somerset
Printed and bound by Professional Book Supplies, Oxford, England

CONTENTS

ACKNOWLEDGEMENTS

Many people on both sides of the Atlantic helped me with this book, and I would like to thank them all for their continual support. To Karen Kincaid at the Algonquin Hotel, Vincent Sardi, the Waldorf Astoria, the Plaza Hotel, the Cafe des Artistes, to Dan Poole at the Players, to L Hardee at The Lambs Club, to the Friars and to Robert Kimball. In London, many thanks to Dianne Coles at Ocean Books for her expert guidance; to Barry Morse for his knowledge and help. Barry, born in Britain, spent many years in the USA on Broadway, in TV and films, and he was the co-founder of the now multi-million dollar "Shaw Festival" at Niagara-on-the-Lake. He is president of the Shaw Society in London. To Paul Webb for his research and work, to Jane Tatam and Bernard McGinley for their advice — and I am deeply thankful to my family, to Gerald who sorted out all the notes, and without whose help this book would have been finished in half the time, and to Colman for his computer expertise.

If you would like to reach the author to find out more about her series of theatre books, please look at the website:

http://www.geocities.com/ colman/guide.html

LIST OF ILLUSTRATIONS

Photo acknowledgements

Pictures numbered 1, 2, 3, 4, 6 and 16 are reprinted here by kind permission of Alexander H Cohen; picture numbered 5 by kind permission of the RSC; pictures numbered 8, 10 and 11, by kind permission of the Redgrave family; pictures numbered 12, 14 & 15 by kind permission of Mander and Mitchenson.

FOREWORD

BY SHERIDAN MORLEY

Once again Elizabeth Sharland has managed to combine theatrical and social history in, so far as I know, the first-ever inclusive account of the Brits on Broadway, what the invasion did both to the invaders and the invaded. At a time when, after a couple of decades in apparent slumber, the New York theatre has again awoken to its own native musical and dramatic talent, it is good to be reminded of the years when it was, amazingly, the British who were essentially keeping the fabulous invalid on a life-support machine.

This is the story of how, for a brief shining moment, Leicester Square got to Times Square.

(Sheridan Morley is the drama critic of the *Spectator* and the *International Herald Tribune* and he writes a regular London newsletter in the New York *Playbill* theatre programmes.)

PREFACE

There have been, over the years, a number of sensational British invasions of the US theatrical scene. As far back as 1820, Edmund Kean electrified American audiences, and besides being paid far more highly than any other performer had even been, he became an honorary Chief of the Huron Indians.

Then in 1849 there were the horrendous Astor Place riots in New York City, arising from simultaneous productions of Macbeth, with the title role being played by the visiting English actor William Macready at the Astor Place Theatre, and by his bitter rival Edwin Forrest at the Bowery. In the ensuing chaos twenty-two people were killed and thirty-six injured.

But in terms of audience enthusiasm and public excitement there is no event in US theatre history to compare with the visit of Charles Dickens in 1867/8 to present readings of his works. The scenes of hysteria at his performances and the riots among people trying to get tickets, were more sensational than the wildest excesses of Beatlemania or the antics of the hyped-up fans of the latest pop megastar.

Dickens was always devoted to the theatre; as a youth he spent much of his very limited pocket money on play-going and, but for a series of flukes of the kind that can channel and divert all our lives, he might well have pursued an acting rather than a writing career.

His meteoric success as an author in the UK was swiftly matched in the US although his material rewards from the States were severely curtailed by the widespread piracy brought about by loose copyright laws. Before he was thirty the serialised chapters of his novels had come to have an addictive fascination for the public as strong as today's TV soap operas.

The death of Little Nell in *The Old Curiosity Shop* had a profound effect on Dickens himself, but even more on his readers, many of whom confessed to having been brought to uncontrollable tears. The Irish MP, Daniel O'Connell, was in a train when he read the chapter. He broke into sobs and flung the book from the carriage window, crying, "He should not have done it." When the ship carrying copies of the last chapters of the story was approaching the pier at New York harbour, there were crowds on the waterfront shouting to those on board, "Is Little Nell dead?"

By the time Dickens came to present his readings in the US he was the most famous author and one of the most famous people in the world. He had begun readings from his works nearly fifteen years earlier, to raise funds for various charities. They had been immensely successful and led to his touring the UK on his own account (despite the misgivings of some of his more snobbish friends who felt it was not quite "gentlemanly" for him to exhibit himself in this way); but quite apart from enjoying the financial benefits, Dickens was moved by a kind of response from the public that no author had ever enjoyed before: it was warm, it was tangible, and it was immediate. He could not resist it, despite the sapping of his strength and the damage to his health.

When he arrived in the States there were extraordinary scenes as people strove to get tickets. Days before sales began there were hundreds camping in the streets with blankets and mattresses in the bitter winter weather, and waiters from neighbouring restaurants and bars providing a running food and drinks service. Riots broke out, only partly controlled by club-wielding police, when speculators tried to infiltrate the line-up. Touts acquired and sold tickets at scores of times their face value.

Dickens gave seventy-six performances and they produced unprecedented demonstrations of enthusiasm; cheers and tears and standing ovations everywhere; but on Dickens himself they imposed a heavy toll. He had constantly to seek medical help and travelled with a chest of medications including laudanum and a form of digitalis. His manager had often to revive him with brandy during intermissions and sometimes he would lie prostrate on a sofa for half an hour at the end of the evening. Even so, he never missed a performance, and, before his last reading in New York, managed to attend and speak at a huge farewell banquet at Delmonico's. When he embarked on the ship that was to carry him back to England, a whole convoy of tugs, steamboats and police tenders followed it down the Bay, saluting with whistles and cannons, Dickens himself meanwhile, standing on the deck, waving his hat on the end of his cane and shouting, "Goodbye, God bless you, everyone."

During the twentieth century many other theatrical adventurers from Britain have made their mark on Broadway. In this fascinating guide Elizabeth Sharland follows on from her best-selling book on historic theatrical London with a similar approach to the British theatrical heritage of New York

INTRODUCTION

This is a short guide to New York's historic theatreland with a look at some of the famous places where the legendary British performers worked, where they stayed, and where they were wined and dined by the old style impresarios and their American counterparts. It includes three walks through Manhattan, and in the postscript I suggest where British actors could do showcases, and playwrights try out their plays if they carry their scripts with them across the pond.

It is not a comprehensive history of every British production, as one can take only so many glittering openings, names of plays and performers. Up to the time when Hugh (Binkie) Beaumont was still running the West End, the transfer of a play to New York was something special. During recent years, literally dozens of British actors have worked in New York and Brooklyn.

The Royal Shakespeare Company, the Royal National Theatre, the Almeida and Donmar Warehouse productions have made many successful tours, and every performer has their own story about the experience. Robert Stephens (late ex-husband of Maggie Smith), in his autobiography, *Knight Errant*, co-written with Michael Coveney, said that if you are successful in New York, the world is your oyster, and everyone is after you. Albert Finney once told him that when he was in a play on Broadway, he received a phone call from a well-known actress in California, who said that she was coming to see the play, and then to see him afterwards. He had never met her in his life. She flew into New York, saw the play, saw Albert, took him to bed and then flew home again. Stephens said that nobody actually flew that far for a night in bed with him, but that he was propositioned by Marlene Dietrich at a party in New York.

In those days actors were invited to sophisticated, elegant parties after the show, and somehow the glamour of these receptions seemed to be a kind of reward for all the days spent in London when unemployed - living in damp cold bedsits with missing bathrooms, existing on baked beans. Actors were taken very seriously in the 50s. People would queue for seats all day, sometimes overnight, to see Olivier, Richardson or Burton. Robert Stephens said that New York was marvellous fun.

John Lahr, the theatre critic, said Broadway is the nostalgia for a theatrical universe that no longer exists. "The real theatre, the theatre that takes us further into ourselves and into the world hasn't happened on Broadway for thirty years."

As the twentieth century rushes to a close, perhaps we can call everything that happened during it historical. It makes little sense to write a British theatrical guide to New York if all the performers, places and shows are too far back. Great performances of Sir Henry Irving, Ellen Terry, Booth etc. make us wonder if they would still raise interest in a theatre-going public. One cannot know their work at first hand, so it might be better to start with a guide that revives memories of people who are still remembered personally. Within a lifetime we see many performers and can therefore make comparisons. Noel Coward is more recent than Oscar Wilde, Laurence Olivier and Richard Burton than Irving and Tree. Christopher Plummer brought to life the personality of Barrymore in his one-man show on Broadway in the 1990s, so legends are sometimes kept alive. One-man shows about Oscar Wilde and Bernard Shaw will no doubt continue to re-acknowledge their genius, but it is with their personalities that the greatest contemporary interest exists. Although traditions about Irving, Terry and Beerbohm Tree are still current in the English theatre, when people go to New York they are more interested in seeing places where the later generations of actors celebrated and partied with their counterparts in New York.

Many English actors get a sense of new and liberating possibilities for themselves on arriving in America. In England, it is all much smaller and more serious.

Up to the 1950s most theatre people travelled by ship to New York. George Arliss in his book, *Up from Bloomsbury,* records how ill he was with sea-sickness on board the *Campania.* George C Tyler had hired him at the last minute, he says, to tour America in a company headed by Mrs Patrick Campbell. He advises that you never take your steward's word when he says, "You'll feel better on deck." Those transatlantic crossings must have been very glamorous if you were travelling in first-class.

George Arliss had a vivid memory, as the ship left England, of Gerald du Maurier waving him farewell. Du Maurier had decided not to leave England, and he became the most popular actor in London. Arliss did not dream it would be more than twenty years before he played another season in London.

Noel Coward crossed to New York in 1920; he was just twenty-one. He has written about his numerous voyages across to America, and of how he managed to meet many influential people on board. Most British actors mention the number of friends they have made on ships, and Laurence Olivier was another who crossed many times, but not only to Broadway. He wrote, "I'm sure that if Beverly Hills had been around for Burbage, Garrick, Kean and Irving, they would have boarded a fast ship to the

New World before breakfast." Both Gielgud and Olivier were inspired by John Barrymore's Hamlet, and Olivier says that when Barrymore was on stage, the sun came out— "Barrymore affected all our generation for a time." He added that Barrymore was the direct link with Edwin Booth, "The Prince of Players". Booth's father was a contemporary of Kean. Booth and Kean actually performed together, alternating the roles of Iago and Othello, both in Britain and America.

Not only did British actors admire their counterparts in New York but they were also impressed with the productions. Coward writes that he was amazed at the speed of the actors' delivery. The pace of a comedy was much faster than of plays in London.

Olivier too was astonished at the difference. Audiences seem to be educated to grasp the plots, comedy lines and fast pace, and took for granted the snappy dialogue. Coward was inspired by the brilliance of Lynn Fontanne and Alfred Lunt, and worked closely with them for many years, eventually writing his play, *Design for Living*, for them. To see them on stage was mesmerising. There was a magic between them that was unique, similar to the same combination found between Coward and Gertie Lawrence. Mrs Patrick Campbell remarked of Coward's dialogue: "His characters talk like typewriting," which leads to another quotation from Alexander Woolcott about her. After her Hollywood debut a few years before she died he said, "She is like a sinking ship firing on its rescuers." Her popularity diminished in New York because of her outlandish behaviour. She insulted managers on and off stage, and once when she was playing in a comedy of Ivor Novello's in New York, she insisted on including ("interpolating" was Gielgud's word) a speech from Electra in the middle of a scene.

New York is one chapter in Gielgud's book, *Distinguished Company*. He says he arrived in 1928 to act in a play that only ran one week. Even then the Hotel Algonquin was packed with celebrities. He writes that he loves the brilliant quality of the New York lights - the vista of Fifth Avenue from St Patrick's Cathedral to the Plaza Hotel is one of the finest sights in the world, better than Bond Street as it used to be.

CHAPTER ONE

THE GREAT WHITE WAY

Although it is exhilarating to arrive in New York by sea, passing the Statue of Liberty and the skyscrapers of Manhattan by the harbour, it is an unforgettable sight to fly in at night. If you are fortunate enough to fly over the city on a clear crisp night, the whole area is lit up for many miles around. Flying just above the top of the Empire State Building is breathtaking; you are looking at illuminations of immense proportions, floodlit skyscrapers, golden rows of lights far below and Broadway, an even brighter glow, cutting right across the patterns of lights. The skyscrapers are like shimmering columns rising from a bed of sparkling lights, forming a huge carpet.

No wonder they call it The Great White Way. It's like seeing a huge fireworks display upside down as the plane slowly descends. It must be one of the most spectacular sights in the world, and somehow you can feel the electricity rising up spiritually to greet you. The city that never sleeps is laid out underneath you.

The Great White Way is, of course, Broadway. It is interesting to note that the theatre district we know today, that is from around West 42nd Street up to the 50s, is not where the theatreland originally started on Broadway. Theatreland moved up town as Manhattan grew. The Astors and wealthy New Yorkers built their mansions uptown, so the theatres moved too.

Let's take just one example, the Broadway Theatre itself. The first-named Broadway Theatre was built at 356 Broadway, a long way from the present one which is at 1681 Broadway. The original was built in 1847; it was modelled on London's Haymarket Theatre built at that time. The next Broadway theatre was built in 1888 at 41st Street. Both Henry Irving and Edwin Booth made their final appearances there. It was used later as a movie theatre before being pulled down in 1929. The Broadway now stands on Broadway at 53rd Street. It has been part of the Shubert empire since 1943.

By 1874 the theatre district had moved from the Wall Street area to Broadway between Union and Herald Squares. J Lester Wallack's theatre, at 13th and Broadway, played classy French and English farces; opera reigned on 14th Street at The Academy of Music, while Booth's theatre at

1

the south-east corner of 6th Avenue and 23rd Street provided stars both domestic and foreign, including, of course Shakespeare. Charlotte Cushman was the great actress in those days.

In 1895 impresario Oscar Hammerstein 1 erected on the west side of Broadway between 44th and 45th Streets the mammoth Olympia Theatre. He was thought mad. Thomas Edison in the 1880s had strung his electric lights along Broadway, giving it a new nickname, "The Great White Way", but only as far north as 42nd Street, and the dark area north of there was known as the "Thieves Lair". Who would venture there to attend a play? The wags were proved correct. The Olympia closed two years later, leaving its owner bankrupt. When John Barrymore's father Maurice saw Hammerstein's new enormous theatre, he quipped, "Here is a theatre where one may be obscene and not heard."

If Henry Irving and Ellen Terry were the royal dynasty of the British theatre at the beginning of this century, then the Drew-Barrymores were the royal dynasty in New York. As has been written, the Barrymores were the unrivalled royal family of a kingdom called Broadway.

Maurice Barrymore (1847-1905) came from a theatrical family, and his three children, Ethel, John and Lionel, followed in his footsteps; all of them became famous, and the next generation also. John Barrymore married Evelyn Nesbit, then Irene Fenwick who later married Lionel. Ethel Barrymore was the first of the three to become famous. She went to England to act with Irving and then worked for the Broadway producer, Charles Frohman. She was named "The Glamour Girl", and became the darling of society. Winston Churchill, as well as several millionaires, proposed to her, but she turned them all down saying, "My world is the theatre."

As London had Charles Cochran and Binkie Beaumont with top stars and directors, so too did New York. Jed Harris produced a play which made him famous overnight. The Royal Family was a satire based on the Barrymore dynasty, and Broadway produced with George Abbott was another hit. He produced *The Green Bay Tree* with Laurence Olivier playing a kept homosexual, and also produced Thornton Wilder's *Our Town*, and *The Heiress*, based on Henry James's novel, *Washington Square*.

George Abbott called Jed Harris "The Little Napoleon of Broadway". He had the reputation of being a wild, ill-mannered, cruel man with a biting sarcastic tongue. Ruth Gordon wrote a blistering report about him in her autobiography. She was fortunate to have a role written for her by Thornton Wilder as Dolly Levi in *The Matchmaker*. She was the first American actress cast in an Old Vic production as Mrs Pinchwife in *The Country Wife*.

George Abbott, already mentioned, became a legend and he kept producing plays well into his nineties. In 1994 Abbott received the Distinguished Achievement in Musical Theatre Award from the Drama League, and in his honour the Mr Abbott Award is given annually by the Society of Stage Directors and Choreographers.

He produced, co-authored and play-doctored for over seventy years. He staged Richard Adler's *Damn Yankees*, *The Pajama Game*, and many famous shows were dubbed with the "Abbott Touch", meaning he kept the shows spinning at a brisk pace throughout, his only request being, he said, that the actors must "say their final syllables".

The Olympia was only a moment ahead of its times. At Longacre Square, the *New York Times* erected its new skyscraper. The intersection was re-christened Times Square. On New Year's Eve 1905, with searchlights ablaze on the brilliant new tower and lighting up the sky, it witnessed a crowd of thousands spontaneously arriving upon the scene to ring in the New Year and celebrate the opening of Times Square. Thus began a tradition that continues to this day. At the same moment Times Square became the centre of New York and of its theatre district. Between 1900 and 1930, eighty-five theatres were constructed, and this area became the largest and most concentrated theatre centre in the world. In 1931 the famous Art Deco Edison Hotel was built on 47th Street, and America's great inventor, Thomas Edison, turned on the lights on opening day by remote control from his home in New Jersey. Many British stars stayed there, and it is worth a visit to see the great Art Deco designs that still exist today.

Then the great producers followed to run all these theatres. Their names are legendary. Many of them went to London and brought back British shows and performers. Mention must be made of them as they started the British invasion in its modern sense. Here is a short list.

Charles Frohman, 1860-1915

He was one of the most famous New York producers of all time. His two brothers, Daniel and Gustave were also in the theatre. In 1893 he founded the Empire Theatre Stock Company, with John Drew as his leading actor. He was well aware of the importance of having stars, whom he promoted and sent on tours. From 1896 he started production at The Duke of York theatre in London with a similar emphasis. The following year in New York he was one of the founders of the Theatrical Syndicate, which virtually monopolised theatre production in New York. He produced Oscar Wilde's *The Importance of being Ernest* in 1895, and J M Barrie's *The Little Minister*. He read J M Barrie's novel, *The Little Minister*, and wanted it made into a play. Barrie said, "He wanted me to be a playwright, but I really wanted to write novels." He also produced Barrie's *Peter Pan* in New York in 1899 and in London in 1904.

George Bernard Shaw said of Frohman: "He was the most wildly romantic and adventurous man of my acquaintance. He has become the most famous manager through his passion for putting himself in the way of being ruined."

He brought over the actress Billie Burke who promptly fell in love with and married Florenz Ziegfeld. Barrie asked him to sail to England to discuss his play, *Peter Pan*. He died tragically in 1915 when the *Lusitania* went down.

His brother, Daniel Frohman, (1851-1940) developed the system of "auxiliary road companies" which toured while the original cast continued playing in New York. He was manager of the Lyceum Theatre from 1887 to 1909. Like his brother, Charles, he produced works by Barrie and Wilde, but also plays by Sardou, Pinero and Henry Arthur Jones.

George Tyler, 1867-1946

He first brought over the Irish Players from the Abbey Theatre in Dublin, who caused a near riot when they opened with Synge's *Playboy of the Western World*. He also produced in New York Sean O'Casey's *The Plough and the Stars* (1927). He brought over Mrs Patrick Campbell and Eleanora Duse. He became the mentor of the child actress Helen Hayes, and discovered the young Lynn Fontanne. He preferred to produce new works rather than revivals, and brought many actors from Britain and France to the United States.

David Belasco, 1853-1931

He built the Belasco Theatre at 111 West 44th Street in 1907. He did forty-two original productions and was famous for *The Darling of the Gods* and *The Girl of the Golden West*. He wrote seventy plays and collaborated with De Mille on some of these works. He pioneered the use of electric lights to create mood. Tony Randall's new classical repertory company, the National Actors Theatre, was housed in the Belasco in 1991.

The Shubert Brothers

Sam, Lee and Jacob began their careers in the late nineteenth century. During the 1910s and 1920s they built many of the Broadway theatres. In addition they came to own and operate more than one hundred theatres across the United States and to book more than a thousand others.

Today the Shubert organisation combines business with theatrical real estate and a production company. Since 1972 two former lawyers of the Shuberts, Gerald Schoenfeld and Bernard B Jacobs, have run the business.

They introduced the computerised ticketing system, and have been influential in the revitalisation of the Times Square area.

Oscar Hammerstein I, 1847-1919

He was an immigrant from Prussia, and became rich in the first place from the cigar business, then switched to theatre. He built the Manhattan Opera House and later sold it to the Metropolitan Opera. His Victoria Theatre opened in 1899 as a legitimate theatre, but owing to the competition from Charles Frohman's Theatrical Syndicate decided to convert it to a vaudeville theatre which, under the management of his son Willie, became the most successful vaudeville house in the United States. His sobriquet, The Father of Times Square, derived from the fact that his Victoria Theatre was the first to be built there, at the time well north of the theatre district.

Oscar Hammerstein II, 1895-1960

He was the son of the above, becoming the foremost writer of lyrics for musicals in his day. *Rose-Marie*, for which he wrote the lyrics, was first produced in 1924, and catapulted him to fame. *The Desert Song* followed in 1926, and in 1927 came *Show Boat* with the score by Jerome Kern, lyrics by Hammerstein. His collaboration with Richard Rodgers in 1943 resulted in *Oklahoma, Carousel, South Pacific, The King And I, Flower Drum Song*, and, in 1959, *The Sound Of Music*.

George M Cohan, 1878-1942

Performer, playwright, director and producer, he opened his own theatre in 1911. He lived at the Hotel Knickerbocker on the corner of 42nd Street and Broadway. His life story was filmed in 1942 (*Yankee Doodle Dandy* with James Cagney), and you can see a statue of him which was erected in 1959, in Duffy Square next to the Half-Price Ticket booth. A musical based on his career, *George M*, was produced on Broadway in 1968. He was known as Mr Broadway and it is interesting to see a plaque in his honour in the Oak Room at the Plaza Hotel, in the alcove where he used to dine. His songs are still well-known, including *Yankee Doodle Dandy*, and *Forty-five Minutes from Broadway*. J McCabe wrote a book, *George M Cohan, The Man who owned Broadway*, in 1973.

Alexander H Cohen

He has just completed a run of his one-man show, *Star Billing*, in New York, and here is a list of credits billed in the program. He is notable in the theatre as one of the last producers of quality productions willing to take significant risks while at the same time maintaining a high ratio of success. Among his Broadway presentations: the NY Drama Critics Circle Award-winning play, *Home*, by David Storey, starring Sir John Gielgud and Sir Ralph Richardson, directed by Lindsay Anderson; the Tony Award-winning Harold Pinter drama, *The Homecoming*, directed by Peter Hall; Jules Feiffer's *Little Murders*; Peter Brooks' Tony Award-winning *La Tragedie de Carmen*; Ben Kingsley as Edmund Kean; Eugene O'Neill's *Anna Christie* starring Liv Ullmann, directed by Jose Quintero; *Comedians* by Trevor Griffiths, directed by Mike Nichols, and introducing Tony Award winner, Jonathan Pryce; James Joyce's *Ulysses in Nighttown*, starring Zero Mostel, directed by Burgess Meredith; Anne Bancroft and Jason Robards in John Whiting's *The Devils*, directed by Michael Cacoyannis; Angela Lansbury in her Tony Award-winning performance in *Dear World*, Jerry Herman's adaptation of Giraudoux's *The Madwoman of Chaillot*; *The School For Scandal*, co-starring Sir John Gielgud and Sir Ralph Richardson; *Hamlet* starring Richard Burton; Chekhov's *Ivanov* starring Sir John and Vivien Leigh; Dario Fos' *Accidental Death of An Anarchist* starring Jonathan Pryce; Walter Slezak in Tyrone Guthrie's production of *The First Gentleman*; Louis Calhern as King Lear in a production directed by John Houseman with music by Marc Blitzstein, as well as *A Day in Hollywood, A Night In the Ukraine*, directed by Tommy Tune (Tony Award); *84 Charing Cross Road*, starring Ellen Burstyn; Peter Shaffer's *Black Comedy* directed by John Dexter, which introduced Michael Crawford and Lynn Redgrave to Broadway; *6 Rms Riv Vu*, starring Jerry Orbach and Jane Alexander; and the Sherlock Holmes musical, *Baker Street*, directed by Harold Prince. He co-sponsored, with LaMaMa ETC, the Peter Brook productions of *The Conference of the Birds*, *Ubu Roi*, and *The Ik*, as well as the Broadway revivals of O'Neill's *Long Day's Journey Into Night* and *Ah, Wilderness*, both starring Jason Robards and Colleen Dewhurst.

He originated a novel idea of producing plays at nine p.m. instead of eight p.m. His *Nine O'clock Theatre* had ten successive hits, commencing with Michael Flanders and Donald Swann in *At the Drop of A Hat*, followed by *An Evening with Mike Nichols and Elaine May*; *Beyond the Fringe*; *Yves*

Montand; the revivals of Sir John Gielgud's *Ages of Man* and Victor Borge's *Comedy in Music*; plus *At the Drop of Another Hat, Maurice Chevalier at 77, Marlene Dietrich*; and *Good Evening*, starring Peter Cook and Dudley Moore. He also presented *Words and Music*, starring Sammy Cahn and the tour of Lena Horne's *Nine O'clock Revue*.

In London, Mr. Cohen has offered West End playgoers a variety of successes including Arthur Miller's *The Price*; Neil Simon's *Plaza Suite*; Robert Morley in Peter Ustinov's *Halfway Up the Tree*, directed by Sir John Gielgud; Charles Boyer in Terence Rattigan's *Man and Boy*; James Stewart in *Harvey*; three Haymarket Company revivals starring Sir Ralph Richardson; Shakespeare's *Merchant of Venice*, Shaw's *You Never Can Tell*, and Sheridan's *The Rivals*; John Mortimer's *Come As You Are*; Peter Ustinov in *The Unknown Soldier and His Wife*; and the musicals, *1776* and *Applause*, starring Lauren Bacall.

He originated the Tony Award telecasts in 1967 and for twenty years the flamboyant showman make this annual "Rite of Spring" the liveliest and most entertaining of the various award shows, while stirring interest in the Broadway theatre throughout America and abroad. He is partnered with Hildy Parks, sole writer of more than forty prime-time network specials. The team also produced the three television specials for Liza Minnelli, Placido Domingo, and Marlene Dietrich. They have produced the Emmy Awards three times (once for each network) as well as the Grand Opening of the Disney MGM Studios in Orlando, Florida.

Roger Berlind

He has been a theatrical producer for twenty-two years. He sees about a hundred shows a year including show in the States and London. He has been criticised for importing so many shows from London to Broadway.

He is personally involved in productions, reads scripts, attends auditions and rehearsals, takes a direct interest in the writing and the mechanics of advertising and ticket sales. He gambles his own money, especially if a show seems at first sight to be unlikely to make money.

Shows he has been involved in include *Amadeus, City of Angels, Guys and Dolls* (revival of), Stephen Sondheim's *Getting Away with Murder*, and he plans to bring from London in 1999, *Closer* by Patrick Marber, and *Amy's View* by David Hare. The following season he intends to produce two musicals, a revival of *Kiss me Kate*, and *Wise Guys*, a new musical by Stephen Sondheim.

For all his passion for, and involvement in, the creative process, he firmly believes that theatre, including musicals, will die on Broadway unless some better ways are found to control costs of production.

Robert Whitehead

Whitehead was born in Canada, began his producing career in 1947 with *Medea*, starring Judith Anderson. He has had more than fifty New York productions. He is married to the Australian actress, Zoe Caldwell who starred in Medea in 1982. He also produced her in *Lillian*, a play about Lillian Hellman.

A good many inconveniences attend play-going in any large city, but the greatest of them is usually the play itself.
   Kenneth Tynan, *New York Herald Tribune*, 17th February 1957

I didn't like the play, but then I saw it under adverse conditions - the curtain was up.

Groucho Marx

Chapter Two

Charisma in Action

History books tell us about the style of acting in Irving's day. Irving was reported to have been mesmerising. He had that special chemistry and charisma which made him, wherever he was on the stage, the centre. It is interesting to speculate whether we would have called it ham-acting or over-acting if we were to have seen him in our own time.

This unique stage presence is possessed by all great actors. It is something similar to great physical beauty for an actress, which keeps the eye on that performer, and only a very few are blessed with it. In my own lifetime I have witnessed this phenomenon, in Laurence Olivier and in Richard Burton. One watched only them when they came on stage. Burton could have his back to the audience, listening to another actor's speech, but still all eyes were on him.

The saddest part in writing about these actors is that both are dead, so we search for present-day actors who possess this rare quality. Ian McKellen and Kenneth Branagh have that combination of acting talent and chemistry with the audience that gives them command of the stage.

Laurence Olivier captured Broadway when the Old Vic company made the triumphant tour to New York just after the last war, in 1946. The cast list, perhaps the most illustrious in history, was headed by Olivier, Ralph Richardson, and Alec Guinness. The company was the toast of Broadway, and ever since then British actors have made an indelible mark on the American scene. In Olivier's book, *Confessions of an Actor,* he writes that the 1945-1946 season was the one that "made our names. The reception was as happy as a marriage bell." However they found that the costs in New York were much higher than they had anticipated, and the actors were beginning to get hungry.

Vivien Leigh accompanied him on the tour, and they stayed at the St Regis Hotel on West 55th Street. In his book he says he was worried about finances even though they were taking Broadway by storm. "It was natural for the two of us to stay at the St Regis; it would have been misunderstood if we had sought somewhere more economical." ("God, these English have lost all their standards since the war." — David Selznick did actually say those words about England a year later.) People who saw those performances still remember them vividly. It was the continuation of a love affair between American audiences and the British classical theatre. Most of the productions to follow would be the classics - Shakespeare, Ibsen, Shaw, done by the new National Theatre and the Royal Shakespeare Company.

Olivier was conscious about having the luck of the devil. "I wanted to make something of a name as an actor. I suppose I can say I have," he said in September 1946. "I wanted to have a house in the country ... Now ... I think I can honestly say that I would like to 'give' something to the theatre instead of taking something out of it ... I would like to help found ... a steady and strong Old Vic Company ... so steady and strong that it doesn't matter a bit if either I or Ralph Richardson or anyone else retires from it. Something that stands on its own feet and can tell us both to go to hell."

Academics joined the critics in honouring him during his stay in New York. He received a master of arts from Tufts University in Medford, and his film, *Henry V*, had a gala opening at the City Center Theatre.

The two parts of *Henry IV* opened in May, followed by *Uncle Vanya*, *Oedipus* and *The Critic* at the Century Theatre. The run was quickly sold out, and the price of a theatre ticket was $3.90, being sold by scalpers for $50, unheard of in those days.

Richard Burton started his career in London, and played most of the great Shakespearean roles either at Stratford-on-Avon or at the Old Vic. He could hold the audience in the palm of his hand, and his voice was one of the finest in the British theatre. It is instantly recognisable — even years after his death. He was seduced by Hollywood and Elizabeth Taylor. However, he did continue to act on Broadway, but never returned to the Old Vic or the National. He made several appearances on Broadway before he played Hamlet there in 1964, directed by John Gielgud. His career, like that of many of his Welsh compatriots, was marred by alcohol and women.

His Hamlet was sold out, and the Broadway tradition of a standing ovation for a Brit playing Shakespeare on Broadway was followed. He and Julie Andrews were a fire-cracker combination in *Camelot*, for, although Burton could sing about as well as Rex Harrison, his charisma enchanted everybody. Masses of fans waited for him outside every night, and a story, perhaps true, tells that on one snowy night, he spotted a couple leaving the performance early to grab a cab — he watched them depart and shouted from the stage, "Get one for me too."

A drama producer at the BBC said, "He speaks the English language better than almost anybody else." Richard Harris, a close friend, said "Half of him wanted to be the best actor in the world. The other half didn't care enough."

His Hamlet was a great success on Broadway, as well as his role of King Arthur in *Camelot*. He loved the challenge. "It sounds perverse," he admitted, "but when you're given a perfectly written part, like Hamlet, there's not much you can do with it after the first few performances. The Burton Hamlet is the Burton Hamlet and that's that. But in a show like *Camelot* when the changes are coming thick and fast with the re-writes, all things are possible. You can make something of the part that is yours and yours alone." His co-star, Julie Andrews, was now well-known to Broadway audiences, and her reputation as a world-wide international star was firmly established.

Burton's brother, Graham Jenkins, writes in his biography that he went to New York for Burton's final night in *Camelot*. At the farewell party, Moss Hart, the Broadway director, led the toast. "Great actors like you," he said to Burton, "are born once in a lifetime. You are as big a personality off the stage as on the stage, and you are, in every sense, larger then life. I beg you not to waste your wonderful gifts. You must know you have it in you to be one of the greatest stage actors of this century." His brother continues with the words, "Sadly, this plea was only heard. It was not understood."

When Burton played in Peter Shaffer's play, *Equus*, twelve years later, the celebrated agent Robby Lantz said, "He revitalised not just the play but the whole of Broadway. In what had been a lacklustre season, business picked up all around."

His last appearance on Broadway was with Elizabeth Taylor in Noel Coward's play, *Private Lives*. The pre-opening publicity was enormous, and it was the show business event of the season. However the critics panned the production even though all the performances sold out. In 1984, when he died, at his memorial service, the actor George Segal who was his co-star in the film, *Who's Afraid of Virginia Woolf*, said, "There is nothing in my life that comes close to the experience of working with Richard Burton. We have always known, those of us who act, that he was the best one. He makes us all proud to be actors."

Another Welshman who also had problems with alcohol and women was Dylan Thomas. Burton acted in his radio play, *Under Milk Wood*, several times and he appeared in a reading at the Old Vic with other well-known Welsh actors including Emlyn Williams and Rachel Roberts.

Dylan Thomas worked at the BBC, sometimes freelance and also as a member of the staff. He went to America in 1950 on his first tour, giving readings of his works across the States. He was on his fourth visit when he died in New York of alcoholic poisoning. The Chelsea Hotel (see photo) was where he stayed in Manhattan, and there is a plaque outside the front door in memory of him. His favourite drinking spot was the White Horse Tavern in Greenwich Village, but it was at the Chelsea Hotel where he spent his last days.

John Gielgud, of course, is unforgettable. He was an enormous success on Broadway, both acting and directing. He writes that while it is certainly a great advantage, if one's acting is to remain in people's memories for maybe fifty years or so, it does largely depend on the roles one plays. Charles Hawtrey and Gerald du Maurier were both brilliant artists, but they rarely played very ambitious roles; thus the public scarcely remembers them now they are gone. A New York critic said that he was glad a book had been written about the Lunts as he believed America had forgotten them already.

Many of Gielgud's performances are on film so future generations will remember him.

Robert Morley was another charismatic actor who conquered Broadway. In 1948 he opened at the Martin Beck Theatre in his own play, *Edward My Son*. Brook Atkinson in the New York Times wrote, "He is an actor in the grand manner; imposing and deliberate, with a broad sweep to his style of expression. But on the big surfaces he can give you some exquisitely neat details, for he also witty and droll, a master of satiric inflections. He is downright superb."

Morton Gottlieb was the general manager of the company that was comprised of mostly English actors. Robert began inviting people to his dressing-room for tea. He had two dressing-rooms - this one was by the stage to enable him to make quick changes. On matinee days, during the break he would not only invite Peggy Ashcroft, his co-star, but everybody from dressers to stagehands. He provided the tea and everyone had to take turns to bring cookies and cake. Then the actors in other shows in the area started to come over on matinee days and have tea.

Robert Morley's dressing-room became the secret hot spot during Broadway matinees. Nine years later, Helen Hayes revived the tradition when she was in a production of *Time Remembered* with Richard Burton and Susan Strasberg — except she asked the four musicians who were in the show to go backstage to play for them; it was a full-blown revival. Robert Morley's distinct, brilliant style of comedy will long be remembered.

Elizabeth Taylor also brought great charisma to Broadway. During the time that Richard Burton was playing Hamlet she would go to the theatre every night and be mobbed at the stage door. Hundreds of people would stop traffic in Times Square just to get a glimpse of her. Later she appeared in *The Little Foxes* and, with Burton, in Coward's *Private Lives* on Broadway.

Broadway audiences still remember John Gielgud, Laurence Olivier, Richard Burton, Rex Harrison, Robert Morley as the British stars who captured New York by their charisma.

"The British invasion of Broadway would not have been possible, and would not have succeeded, without the enormous strength and talent of the charismatic producers."

If any play has been produced only twice in three hundred years, there must be some good reason for it.

Rupert Hart-Davis

Shut up, Arnold, or I'll direct the play the way you wrote it.

John Dexter to Arnold Wesker

It's about as long as *Parsifal*, but not as funny.

Noel Coward on *Camelot*

CHAPTER THREE

FAMOUS BRITISH STARS ON BROADWAY

"The neon lights of Broadway lure us like moths. We dash ourselves against them again and again in search of we know not what, until we have crippled ourselves, and in this desperate flight we are abetted or rather exploited by television."

Quentin Crisp, *Resident Alien*

It was as early as the 1830s that the British stars went to America, Charles Matthews (1832), Macready (1826-1849), Kean (1830), Charles Kemble and his daughter Fanny (1832), Charles Wyndham (1869), Oscar Wilde (1882, on a lecture tour), Forbes Robertson, Mr and Mrs Kendall, Marie Tempest, Lillie Langtry, H Beerbohm Tree (1882) and Henry Irving (1883, 1904). No company (or actor) was more important in the United States during the nineteenth century than Irving's company. They toured eight times playing most major cities, a total of two hundred and nine weeks. But the legitimate theatre has not been the only attraction. Marie Lloyd, Vesta Tilley and Harry Lauder all made tours in the United States.

In 1879 Gilbert and Sullivan arrived in New York on a Cunard steamship, *Bothnia. The Pirates of Penzance* was premiered there and Sullivan completed it when he was living on East 20th Street. Their main mission however was to stop their work from being illegally produced. Pirate copies of all their comic operas were being performed all over the country as copyright laws had still not been introduced at that time. For *The Pirates of Penzance* they were determined to beat the producer-pirates. Rehearsals were secret, none of the music was printed, and during the entire run the music was collected from the orchestra and locked in a safe each night. Unbelievably, Sullivan, in his hurry, had left some of his music in London and most of the songs for the First Act. The show was to open in a month, and as steamship travel was slow, there was no time to send for them. So he re-wrote all the songs from memory, and scored the entire opera all in one month. Their comic operas were as popular and successful in America as in England.

In the golden era of transfers of British productions to New York, when Binkie Beaumont was still running the West End, there were many great performers who were tempted to stay in America and go to Hollywood, some went for a short while but then returned home. Gladys Cooper was one star who did go to live in Hollywood, but regularly worked on both sides of the Atlantic, and returned to New York to appear in Enid Bagnold's *The Chalk Garden* in 1955 in which she also made her last stage appearance in London shortly before her death.

In 1954 Julie Andrews went to New York in *The Boyfriend*. Then followed *My Fair Lady* in 1956 and *Camelot* in 1960. She was then whisked off to Hollywood stardom both in musical and non-musical films. Her long-awaited return to Broadway didn't happen till 1995, in a stage version of *Victor/Victoria*, and she received an unprecedented outpouring of affection from critics and audience alike. Julie Andrews says that she was fortunate enough to be in at the very end of that great, golden era on Broadway. But one thing she does agree that has changed for the better is that today one can use body mikes now to help save your voice. When she was playing in *My Fair Lady* for more than three years it was killing, an endurance test., Because of the extreme heat of the summer in New York, theatres must also be air-conditioned, and therefore you have to use a mike to overcome the noise of the machine. Jean Marsh recalls that they asked to have the air-conditioning turned off in the theatre, but then she nearly fainted with the heat. Julie conquered New York and the Broadway musical. Julie says she was unbelievably lucky to be given the role of Liza in *My Fair Lady*, and she says that nowadays the cost of producing a musical on Broadway is astronomical. The amount of money needed to put on a major musical is huge. So the old days are over when whatever was a hit on Broadway would eventually be made into a film, and original musicals conceived for films now are very rare. Once, you could have Astaire and Rogers or Garland suddenly stop and sing a song in a movie. Now there seems to be a demand for more reality, for songs coming from a definite source. *Victor/Victoria* is a good example; the character has a reason to get up and sing, because she's a performer.

Angela Lansbury was a renowned character actress in films in the 1940s, and added lustre with stardom on Broadway before achieving fame on the small screen. Today, in her seventies, she is a vital spirit who relishes each new creative endeavour whether it be on Broadway or in Hollywood.

When Rex Harrison went to New York on his first visit, he said all he could remember was the cold! He didn't have the proper clothes and was freezing most of the time. However, he found "hot" jazz, and it was the period when prohibition had just been lifted. He heard the jazz greats, from Fats Waller and Benny Goodman to Paul Whiteman and Count Basie. He remembers going to a favourite place on West 52nd Street called Jack and Charlie's. Now it's called Twenty-One. He writes in his autobiography that the smart people who go there now probably are quite unaware it used to be a speak-easy, one of the places where you knocked, asked for Joe, and waited for the buzzer to let you in.

Another anecdote he recalls was when the stage-hands weren't allowed to hand out the props, and rehearsals ground to a halt. His director, Tyrone Guthrie, came to the rescue and found a non-union rehearsal hall. He writes: "I can remember vividly seeing this tall, lanky Irishman pushing a handcart with all the props in it, followed by the entire company, all trudging up Fifth Avenue behind him to the rehearsal room."

Rex Harrison's last appearance on stage was on Broadway, in Somerset Maugham's *The Circle*. He said that, "as an English drawing-room comedy of 1921, I can only think that its current success in New York must be due to a tremendous need for Americans to escape from the harsh unmannerly lives they live now into a more gracious atmosphere where charm and civilised behaviour were the norm." He was surprised that the critics didn't call the play a lot of old-fashioned rubbish, but called it verbal chamber music, where most of the credit should go to Maugham. He was delighted when one of the critics wrote that he wasn't sure whether Rex Harrison had invented Maugham, or Maugham had invented Rex Harrison. Rex said of Somerset Maugham's comedies that this frivolous high comedy style still works, even in the last decade of this century.

New York audiences were eager to see the plays by British writers. They welcomed, amongst others, George Bernard Shaw, J B Priestley, Maugham, Terence Rattigan and Noel Coward. However these playwrights did not settle in the States but returned home after their plays were produced. One playwright who did stay on, however, was P G Wodehouse.

P G Wodehouse was born in Guildford. He wrote about the aristocracy, class distinctions, butlers and gentlemen burglars. Although most of his witty lyrics have been almost forgotten now, they were sung by stars such as Bea Lillie and Gertie Lawrence.

He first went to New York in 1904 for a few weeks' holiday, when he was twenty-three. He had just left a tediously boring job in a bank, and in one of his books he wrote: "Why America? I have often wondered about that. Why, I mean, from my earliest years was it America that was always to me the land of romance? It is not as though I had been intoxicated by cowboys or Indians, but I had this yearning to visit America."

That same year Wodehouse became involved with the theatre. He was asked to write an extra lyric for a show in London and his friend, Guy Bolton, knew he had a good ear for music. As a result of a successful song, the actor, Seymour Hicks, offered him a job at the Aldwych Theatre as a lyricist to write extra material when needed for a number of musical comedies, and to adapt verses and songs. A friend who was with him at the time said, "On leaving the stage door, Wodehouse was so stunned with joy and excitement that we walked a mile along the Strand without him knowing where he was or whether he was coming or going." The composer he was to work with was Jerome Kern, and thus began a collaboration some years later of Kern and Wodehouse.

After 1909 he travelled regularly to New York. He wrote a play called *A Gentleman of Leisure*, and the gentleman burglar, the lead, was Douglas Fairbanks Sr. It was the first play of its kind that was set on both sides of the Atlantic.

In 1915 he was in New York and met up again with Jerome Kern and Guy Bolton. They became a team and produced an incredible run of hit shows. They were the toast of Broadway, Wodehouse's work was praised to the skies, and his lyrics composed at this time included the famous song, *Bill*, from *Showboat*. Wodehouse became the theatre critic for *Vanity Fair* and Dorothy Parker succeeded him. She wrote: "You could get a seat for their hit show, *Oh, Lady, Lady!* for just about the price of one on the Stock Exchange."

Besides *Oh Lady, Lady!* there were seven or eight other hit shows including *Oh Boy* (1917) renamed *Oh Joy* in London, with Beatrice Lillie, and *Oh Kay* with Gertie Lawrence. George and Ira Gershwin wrote the music and lyrics for this one but they wrote the book and also part of *Anything Goes*. *Oh Kay* was a hit on both sides of the Atlantic.

It is interesting to note the way he worked with Jerome Kern. Wodehouse said that Jerome usually wrote the music first and then he would add the words. "That way he can see which are the musical high spots in it, and can fit the high spots to the lyric." W S Gilbert, of Gilbert and Sullivan fame, argued with this and said the words should come first. Wodehouse's talent was not in writing lyrics which read as light verse but fitting the words to the tune.

Unfortunately such musical comedies are no longer produced, but Broadway still remembers those hits. Ira Gershwin, Cole Porter, Noel Coward all recognised his unique style, although hardly any of his lyrics survived.

Wodehouse was criticised for being in America during the 1914-1918 war; however, he had trouble with his eyes, which excused him although his public did not know this fact. His greatest successes were in New York in the 1920s, and people such as Noel Coward and Gertie Lawrence would have been vastly impressed with the huge successes he was having. He crossed the Atlantic frequently, to enable him to work on the productions both in New York and London.

His nick-name was Plum, and in January 1929 his daughter wrote an article about him for the *Strand Magazine*, saying that he had an overwhelming horror of being bored, and an overpowering hatred of hurting people.

It is unusual that a writer whose subjects seem so much attuned to British readers should have so much success in America. However, the Americans have always had an interest in British writing. The common language, the fact that historically the Americans were of British stock, and the traditional colonial inferiority complex, made many of them consider work emanating from England superior to what was written in the United States. The turn-of-the-century habit of US heiresses marrying English aristocrats is another example of this veneration of their English roots.

Wodehouse might have appealed because his writing is a put-down of English superiority; his aristocrats are buffoons, his Jeeves is like Barrie's Admirable Crichton, in that he is cleverer, more realistic than his master. His London club The Drones, for example, is not one that an intelligent American would aspire to. In fact, the whole English social scene is farcical, a sort of never-never land of unmerited affluence and ease, with trivial pre-occupations and pointless activities conducted by mindless idiots, condescended to by their servants.

His style has been often praised to the skies; it is simple, clear, direct and witty in a school-boyish way. It is true that in England his greatest fans have been school-boys, many of whom carried their infatuation into their adult lives. George Bernard Shaw, who was neither English nor a public-school product, had little regard for Wodehouse's work, any more than he did for another school-boy favourite, G K Chesterton. Both Chesterton and Wodehouse were enormously popular with the English middle classes, neither had written anything remotely intellectual, nor, dare one say it, intelligent.

Bertie Wooster is the prototype of the genre of idle young men, living on inherited wealth or allowances from family fortunes, who had nothing worthwhile to do, nor any interest in doing anything worthwhile; Wodehouse's genius was in making such a person a subject for comedy, and his trivial preoccupations, dress, parties and other social engagements, comic. There is no hint of political interest in Wodehouse, he is not even satirical, and his characters, Jeeves and Bertie Wooster, were not drawn from living models; Lord Emsworth is similarly an imaginary but comic figure, made fun of through his obsession with a pig. So it is easy now to understand why he was drawn into recording messages for broadcasting from Germany to America during the second world war.

George Bernard Shaw wrote novels, drama and music criticism for nine years before he became a successful playwright. Two of his plays were produced in New York in the 1890s, and finally he was established, not only in England but in New York. His success came very quickly after constant rejection in Britain. Richard Mansfield, an actor-manager, used to boast that he had made Shaw a fortune. Most of his plays opened in New York shortly after the London openings, and it was only then that Shaw became financially independent. Two of his plays had their world premières in New York - *Heartbreak House* and *St Joan*, then the Theatre Guild presented seven more.

Eugene O'Neill admired Shaw and wrote that his own writing was influenced by him. Additionally, several other US playwrights started to imitate the Shavian themes, including Edward Sheldon who wrote a play called *Salvation Nell*. Shaw received an Academy Award in 1938 for best screen adaptation of his own play, *Pygmalion*, starring Wendy Hiller and Leslie Howard. However one play, *Mrs Warren's Profession*, was viciously attacked and called obscene by the New York press, the cast even being put in jail for a short time; but the ensuing publicity caused a surge at the box office and Shaw became famous.

The Broadway audiences were fully aware of what was happening in London, and when the new kitchen sink dramas of the 50s and 60s became successful, they too went to New York. *Look Back in Anger* transferred, followed by the new plays of Osborne, Storey, Wesker and Alan Bennett. Albert Finney, Tom Courtenay, Alan Bates all found fame on Broadway, and were offered Hollywood contracts, but they wanted to do theatre work, and came back to Britain. They were fortunate enough to get their start when these new playwrights were beginning. "Who wants to carry spears for five years when you could whack the audience between the eyes in a John Osborne or David Storey?"

British playwrights were fortunate enough to have these well-known actors in their plays. Alan Bates and Simon Gray worked well together. Tom Courtenay and Albert Finney had a marvellous success in Ronald Harwood's play, *The Dresser*, and Alan Bennett could get almost any British star to act in his plays. David Hare, who is the most produced living playwright at the National Theatre first started writing in the 1960s. *Plenty* proved one of the most successful exports to Broadway, winning rave reviews and the New York Critics Circle Award. He and Christopher Hampton went to school together, and Hampton's plays were equally successful, although it was one of David Hare's plays, *The Secret Rapture*, that received a bad notice from the New York Times theatre critic, Frank Rich, known as "The Butcher on Broadway". After the review the play closed after nineteen previews and twelve performances. Hare retaliated and wrote back to him. His letter was circulated, attacking Rich for irresponsible nastiness, and for single-handedly closing his play, *Variety*, the show business weekly, hailed Hare's attack under a banner headline: "Ruffled Hare Airs Rich Bitch". They agreed with the playwright, and accused Rich of a spree of negative reviews and sarcastic notices, and of being the cause of increasing resentment in the trade. Hare asked to meet him; Rich wrote back, but refused to meet Hare; "Next time you're in New York, why not spend less time meeting with critics, or attempting to, and more time seeing the plays your audience is seeing. You may learn more about why your play closed." He added, "*The Times* did not close your play ... the producers closed your play."

Rich also panned a production of *The Tempest* with Frank Langella playing the role of Prospero. The director, Jude Kelly, came from Britain with a big reputation, but all the New York critics seemed to agree that her low-key production was a let-down, and lacked the true Shakespearean authority.

Hare's complaint is a common one on Broadway, but it is seldom heard so publicly. Basically the objection is that the *New York Times* is so influential that its critic can close a show. Hare told *Variety*: "I think Rich is totally irresponsible in the use of his power." *Variety* commented "Rich's exceptionally harsh review of the Hare play, which drew favourable reviews from other critics, guaranteed its box office doom."

The Irish playwright, Brendan Behan, visiting New York in connection with the production of *The Hostage* (1969) also was vulnerable to the critics, and he wrote:

> A Broadway author ... I am proud to call myself one ... always waits, on the first night of his play, either in 'Sardi's' or 'Downey's', and his press agent goes out to get the six newspapers, which are called 'the Six Butchers of Broadway'.
>
> Now if you get six out of six good reviews, you could ask the President of the United States to sell you the White House, though I don't think this has ever happened. If you get five good reviews, you are doing fairly well and you have to start worrying about 480 Lexington Avenue, which is the home of

the income tax. It is not a bad kind of worry though in its own way, if you have got to have worries, and I suppose everyone has to have them. If you have four, you can afford to give a party, or at least you can afford to attend the party which is usually given for you.

If you get three good reviews, it's time like to go home to bed, but if you only get two, you stay there, and the whole of the following day and don't go out until after dark. If you get one good review, you just make an air reservation very quickly to get back to where you came from, but if you get six bad reviews, you take a sleeping pill. You might even take an overdose!

However I think I got five or six good reviews. Enough to keep me in business anyway. I know Walter Kerr of the *New York Herald Tribune* and Howard Taubman of the *New York Times* were both enthusiastic over *The Hostage* and they are the really important reviewers. No, I forget. They are all important. I will be writing another play!

Actually, I got pretty good reviews and when I went into 'Sardi's' that night, the crowd stood up and clapped.

In the early 1970s, PBS television started showing *Upstairs Downstairs* and *Brideshead Revisited*, and the among American public there was a terrific surge of interest in British drama. Jean Marsh and Eileen Atkins, who created *Upstairs Downstairs*, became household names over there, and still are, as the series is still airing in many parts of the US

Eileen Atkins had been to America already, and starred in *The Killing of Sister George* in 1967, but she said even at that time that unless a theatre actress were to do TV work in Britain you could not make ends meet. All you do is subsidise the theatre when you work in London, as the salaries are so low. She told a reporter that she felt more glamorous in America, and she was very tempted to stay there. She said there is always a chance there of doing a Shakespeare play for people who don't know how it ends. Along with Rosemary Harris, Zoe Caldwell and Zoe Wanamaker, she gets much of her best work done in New York.

She continued to say that when she comes home and waits for the next job, it nearly always comes from America. In England, whenever you play a part they all remember how Dame Sybil or Edith Evans or Irene Worth used to do it; in America you can say, look, forget everything you know about this play, if anything, start here and now with me. In England you can never get critics or audiences to do that.

She knows that there is a danger of ending up in mid-Atlantic if you try to plan a career in both countries, but it just seems to happen that the best offers come from over there.

"The English are good with words; they're brilliant technicians, but Americans act with guts, so both nationalities benefit from working together."

Eileen Atkins first met Vanessa Redgrave in Stratford in 1955, and they have been close friends ever since. Both Vanessa and Lynn have had successes on Broadway, followed by the younger Redgrave generation, and in the 1990s Eileen Atkins devised a play called *Vita and Virginia* from the letters of Vita Sackville West and Virginia Woolf which was a great hit in New York, starring Vanessa and Eileen, Zoe Caldwell directing.

Jean Marsh had been in New York working as an actress before the TV series, *Upstairs Downstairs*, but she did not have very much work and returned to Britain, only to be "discovered" after the series was aired. In 1979 she starred with Tom Conti on Broadway in *Whose Life is it Anyway?* She had already been seen in 1957 in *Much Ado about Nothing* with John Gielgud.

Even though she had a star role she tells of the cramped backstage conditions. There was a little warren of dressing-rooms. Hers was on the second floor landing of a back stairway, not much bigger than a closet with dreams of grandeur. In 1975 she was in Alan Bennett's *Habeas Corpus* with Rachel Roberts, Donald Sinden, June Havoc and Celeste Holm. However, the New York based British critic Clive Barnes gave it a bad review, and Bennett said that he was glad Barnes doesn't operate in London.

Pauline Collins, another actress who appeared in *Upstairs Downstairs*, was a great success in *Shirley Valentine* on Broadway, and people wanted to see these British actors in the theatre. Jeremy Irons, after his appearance in *Brideshead Revisited*, starred in *The Real Thing*, and was almost on overnight success in becoming a face-recognisable actor when he began his career in feature films. It is ironic to think that all these theatre actors were now finding success in America through the exposure of their work in British television. Judi Dench said she had been acting for years on stage, but it wasn't until after she had done a TV show that people started recognising her in the street. Her TV series, *As Time Goes By*, is now shown regularly on PBS across America.

Michael Crawford, Jimmy Dale, Robert Lindsay were rediscovered in the US and in 1981 Sir Ian McKellen said, on his return from playing Salieri in *Amadeus*, "I can't convey what a hit on Broadway is like. It's overwhelming." He recalls the night when he received his Tony Award for the role. "I came out of the building and a huge scream went up. I looked around to see who they were screaming at, and it was for me." Jane Lapotaire was also there that night receiving her Tony for her brilliant performance as Piaf in Peter Hall's production.

Dianne Rigg went on a six-month tour in 1974 in the National Theatre's modern version of Molière's *The Misanthrope*, which was directed by John Dexter, but she didn't become a celebrity in the US until the TV series *The Avengers* was shown.

British Directors on Broadway

Peter Hall, Richard Eyre, Michael Blakemore, John Dexter and most of the younger directors at the National and RSC have all worked on Broadway. However, there are some American directors who want to work with British actors in New York, and one of the most brilliant of these is Mike Nichols. He has the knack of putting his own spin on a British play, and he has helped to enlarge the reputation of many British performers and playwrights on Broadway. Nichols has since gone on to direct feature films but he got his first start in the theatre when he worked with Elaine May in revue and cabaret work.

Two directors who were working regularly in New York during the 70s and 80s were Peter Hall and John Dexter. Sir Peter still does. In his *Diaries*, first published in 1983, he has many accounts of his productions not only on Broadway but with the Metropolitan Opera Company as well. He juggled new productions on both sides of the Atlantic, between endless meetings and rehearsal schedules, as he was Artistic Director of the National Theatre up till 1988. He directed opera as well as stage plays, not only at Covent Garden and Glyndebourne but across the US as well. His production of *Salome* starring his then wife, Maria Ewing, started in Los Angeles and was seen in Washington, Chicago and San Francisco. In Houston he did the première of Michael Tippet's opera, New Year. Sir Peter seems to possess more energy than any other director on either side of the Atlantic. When Alan Ayckbourn's play, *Bedroom Farce*, transferred to Broadway, American Equity demanded that the British cast be replaced after twelve weeks by an American cast, so Sir Peter had to fly over to

23

audition the Americans actors. He wrote that the American actors treated him like God. "But the very English idiom of Ayckbourn's play really is almost impossible for them. I feel as if I am encouraging them to wear funny hats." In his autobiography he says that rehearsing with talented actors in something he likes to do every day. It is up to me to hold their interest, to inspire them, and I must give unsparingly of my energy. It is almost an erotic passion."

Simon Callow, in his book, *On Being an Actor*, has a brilliant account of his work with Sir Peter and his own role of Mozart in Peter Shaffer's play, *Amadeus*.

The cast of *The Ideal Husband* also had to be recast for its New York run, and many other directors have had the same problem including Michael Blakemore when he recast *Lettice and Lovage*.

When Peter Hall left the National Theatre he formed his own company, The Peter Hall Company, and Richard Eyre took over at the National as Artistic Director.

John Dexter hated working at the National and preferred to remain in New York. He went to New York, after his early career at the Royal Court Theatre with George Devine, where he directed Arnold Wesker's first plays, including *Roots*. It was in this play that Joan Plowright became an overnight success. Dexter continued to direct both in the West End and for Laurence Olivier at the National until he left for New York in 1974. He became the Director of Productions at the Metropolitan Opera as well as directing plays on Broadway including Richard Burton in Peter Shaffer's *Equus*.

He produced opera in New York, sometimes producing the same opera in Europe, in Paris, Zurich and Hamburg. His contribution to the Met was enormous, and he said he was trying to drag opera into the twenty-first century. I quote him - from the cover of a posthumous autobiography: "Fury for perfection makes me difficult to work with." He became known as the "Honourable Beast". The actor, Michael Gambon, said, "If you didn't give your all, he'd have your guts for garters - he was the finest director of the post-war years."

He worked with all the great opera stars who came to the Met during those years. He found a freedom in New York that he hadn't experienced in London. Even though he introduced new techniques and innovative ways of directing, he writes that he used to dream what he called his snob dreams of his twenties. "For the first time," he writes, "I have a sense of belonging with Noel and Larry and all, or at least being up there with them. So from now on I can relax. 'You made it, Avis. Now enjoy it.'" Dexter died during heart surgery in 1990.

The British Invasion has been a subject of intense controversy, reaching a kind of climax with Actor's Equity hesitancy to allow Jonathan Price, the white British star, to play a Eurasian in the musical, *Miss Saigon*. When British stars sign contracts on Broadway, it often means that the next stop is Hollywood. Again, the decision is whether to continue as a stage actor or move into a film career.

Not all visiting thespians have an easy time of it in New York. Reading about and talking to some performers about working there revealed some surprises. Peggy Ashcroft, for example, went over to play in a new American play in 1937 called *High Tor*. Even though Peggy did not like the play it won the New York Drama Critics' Prize for best new play, and had a run for six months. During this time Peggy lived alone in an apartment on Washington Square. She wrote that in New York you "… either sink or swim, and I sank." However it was the play, *The Heiress*, adapted from the Henry James novel, *Washington Square*, that made Peggy famous when she played the lead as Catherine Sloper.

She was very unhappy and began a passionate affair with William Buchan, son of the writer, John Buchan. He wanted to marry her and he returned to London with her. But nothing came of it.

Separation is the name of the game when a play is taken over to Broadway. Show business marriages have to be extremely strong to survive if one partner is working on Broadway and the other is left at home working in a play or tied up with other issues such as children at school or domestic problems.

When Billie Whitelaw went over to play in Samuel Beckett's plays, she was a smash hit. Staying at the Algonquin Hotel, she missed her family desperately. The newspapers, radio and media were clamouring for her, but she said she just wanted to get on with the show and go home. She found the hectic and frantic publicity roundabout quite amazing. It was a sensational success, but the exposure was not something to become addicted to, though many stars welcomed it and came to expect it. In her autobiography she gives a hilarious account of arriving in New York, going to the theatre and finding that she had no dressing-room, and that the theatre was still being built. Nevertheless she got on with it and had great notices.

Judi Dench turned down the chance to go to America with the National Theatre company in 1983, although she had already toured there before her marriage as far as San Francisco. Years before, Ellen Terry said her family meant more to her than the theatre. However she did long tours in America and was able to send them money from there, which probably helped to assuage her anxiety.

In 1958 Olivier arrived in New York with the play, *The Entertainer*, and according to Hugo Vickers in his biography of Vivien Leigh, it was then that his affair with Joan Plowright became serious, as she was in the cast, playing his daughter. Noel Coward had dinner at Sardi's with Olivier after the show one evening during the run on Broadway, and he told Coward he couldn't really take living with Vivien any longer. It was the beginning of the end of the marriage.

After their marriage broke up, Vivien went to New York with the play *Duel of Angels*, and one of the actors in the cast was John Merivale, whom Vivien had met on and off in London. They became seriously involved although they never married; he helped her recover from losing Olivier to Joan Plowright. Robert Helpmann was the director of the play, and he was a close friend who also helped her on both sides of the Atlantic.

Julie Andrews, Rex Harrison and Richard Burton all encountered the problems of family separation, and actors' careers have often been totally changed because of this. Not only did marriages suffer, but when Jessie Matthews went over to New York in Charles Cochran's *Revue 1924*, she went almost as a child. She was wined and dined when touring and during the New York run, so that when she returned to London in sophisticated clothes, in place of the young schoolgirl there was an elegant sophisticated young woman in silk hose, high heels and make-up. As Michael Thornton tells in his biography, her parents blinked in disbelief. "What's the matter with you?" asked her mother. Jessie felt as if she had been slapped in the face. "I suppose we're not good enough for you now," remarked her father.

It is interesting to note the New York audiences often come to expect that British stars who come to Broadway should be in historical plays - if not Shakespeare then something that meets their expectation of a classic British play. Often they are rewarded. Paul Scofield made his New York debut in Robert Bolt's *A Man for all Seasons* in 1961 as Sir Thomas More, Geraldine McEwan in 1963 playing Lady Teazle in Sheridan's *School for Scandal* and so the list goes on. Derek Jacobi, already known from his TV series, *I Claudius*, played in Erdmann's *The Suicide* and Glenda Jackson's debut was in *Marat/Sade* directed by Peter Brook. She later played the lead in the RSC's production of Ibsen's *Hedda Gabler* on Broadway.

Among the most recent have been *Cheek by Jowl*, produced by The Royal Shakespeare Company, the Almeida Theatre's production of *Medea* with Diana Rigg and Ralph Fiennes' *Hamlet*. In 1998 Richard Eyre directed Liam Neeson in David Hare's play, *The Judas Kiss*, and *Amy's View* in 1999.

Many of these actors stayed at the Algonquin Hotel which is a short walk from Broadway, and they were staying in surroundings very much like home. The cuisine used to include all the comfort foods, like rice

1 *Above* Alexander H Cohen with Sir John Gielgud and Vivien Leigh.
2 *Below* Sir John and Sir Ralph Richardson during rehearsals for *Home*.

3 *Above* Alexander H Cohen, Jane Lapotaire, Elizabeth Taylor and Glenda Jackson at the
Tony Awards, New York.
4 *Below* Rex Harrison.

5 *Above* Patrick Stewart.
6 *Right* Richard Burton.
7 *Below* The author with Sir John Gielgud
and Emma Thompson.

8 *Above left* Michael Redgrave with his wife, actress Rachel Kempson.
9 *Above right* Julie Andrews in *The Boyfriend*.
10 *Below left* Lynn Redgrave in *Shakespeare for My Father*.
11 *Below right* Lynn and Vanessa Redgrave in New York.

pudding and steak and kidney pie - meals from an Agatha Christie novel - but a recent complete renovation of the hotel has brought many changes.

The opening night of *Me and My Girl* on Broadway, starring Emma Thompson and Robert Lindsay, was a smash hit. Although Emma Thompson said at the end of the run that if she heard the Lambeth Walk again she'd commit hara-kiri, it had fresh musical vitality, and the Cockney accents lent it a quaint flavour.

Another British "star" on Broadway was the critic, Kenneth Tynan. He became the theatre critic for the *New Yorker* magazine (1958-60) and he championed the new realism of John Osborne and Arnold Wesker. His time in New York is recorded brilliantly in his late wife's biography of him. In 1961 he produced on Broadway *Oh Calcutta*; the all nude show, which shocked most of New York, was nearly closed down by the police but then went on to make millions, although Tynan received only a small percentage. His work as a critic was taken much more seriously. John Lahr was given the same job at the *New Yorker* in 1992 by Tina Brown. He writes: "In American theatrical circles the definition of a genius is anybody from England."

Be that as it may, it is always interesting to wonder why some productions transfer successfully and others fail. When the revue *Beyond the Fringe* with Peter Cook, Dudley Moore, Jonathan Miller and Alan Bennett opened in 1961 it was a great success; however, when Rowan Atkinson's show opened several years ago, it closed within a week.

Alan Bennett (who had been a part author of *Beyond the Fringe*) was another playwright whose plays transferred to New York. *Habeas Corpus* in 1975 starred Donald Sinden in New York and Alec Guiness in London. His first play, *Forty Years On*, starred John Gielgud and together with Peter Shaffer their plays became as popular in America as in Britain.

Looking back, the golden era, the legend of Broadway, really began in the 1920s, when Jack Buchanan, starring in *Between the Devil* with Evelyn Laye and Adele Dixon, was hailed as "The King of Broadway".

CHAPTER FOUR

BROADWAY VERSUS THE WEST END

The main difference between the West End and Broadway is a financial one, and during the past two decades the gap has widened enormously.

The cost of producing a serious straight play in New York is roughly five times as expensive as in London. Several years ago Sam Friedman published a comparison in *The Times*, and announced that Ben Kingsley's one-man show, *Kean*, had cost exactly five times more to stage in New York than in London. In the mid-seventies the unions won excessively generous contracts, and the cost of employing theatre staff became enormous—the curtain man in those days made $549 a week, just to lower and raise the curtain once a night, a hairdresser got $500 a week for one hour's work a day, an understudy got $500 a week, and the actors and producers were caught in a vice-like grip that made them powerless. As a result, production of straight plays plummeted, and no backers would take the chance on a serious new play. The term "the fabulous invalid" was coined and even though the costs were high, it was cheaper to import a British production than to risk producing a new American play on Broadway.

To understand the doubts of the financial backers, you had only to look at the cost sheets. Between sixty to eighty per cent of the cost of a new play went in salaries and royalties. If the overall costs were more reasonable, more producers would take risks with new straight plays.

Even a walk-on part must be paid at a rate four times that which his counterpart in London might receive. The situation is not improving as costs continue to soar. The accusations of feather-bedding are becoming louder, and as the unions still insist in over-staffing theatre jobs, the future looks bleak.

Instead, we are in the era of the multi-million dollar musical, with enormous ticket prices to cover the costs. Where are the smaller straight plays that provoke argument, controversy and inspire? They cannot find backers, nor can Shakespeare. As Benedict Nightingale writes: "One can't imagine *King Lear* being presented at all on Broadway - and that would be first and foremost for reasons of finance."

Joe Papp tried to beat the system by putting some of his smaller theatres into a special category when they housed straight dramas, but stars on

Broadway can command huge salaries, and it is said that Ben Kingsley grossed a weekly $12,500 from *Kean*. Part of the solution would be to have more government money for the American theatre, and the founding of one large permanent repertory company. London has the RSC and the National, but how can Broadway afford to do Shakespeare? - a play with twenty-five characters? It is difficult to understand, with a history of great actors such as Booth, Barrymore and, more recently, Orson Welles, that they have so few chances to offer a single production of the classics or Shakespeare in today's theatre.

Tennessee Williams once said that the theatre had fallen into the receivership of businessmen and gamblers. Today he probably would have been shocked to see the strength that the unions have used to cripple the industry.

Some American playwrights are now going to London to have their new plays produced because the costs are lower and the risks not as great. One newspaper theatre critic in London does not have the power to close a play as in New York. Arthur Miller, for one, has his new plays premièred in London, and other playwrights are following his example.

There are three kinds of commercial theatres in London. First there are musicals which always seem to attract tourists and residents alike, whether it is native or an import from Broadway: second, the straight play with perhaps a well-known celebrity in it, or by a celebrated playwright: thirdly, the theatre for serious thespians, the Royal Shakespeare Company, the National, and often there are new plays by unknown playwrights. Then there is a fourth level - comprised of the non-commercial fringe theatres.

It is roughly the same in New York, where you can have the Broadway musical, the new straight play with a Redgrave or Maggie Smith in it, and dozens of serious theatres from Off/Off Broadway, such as Joe Papp's Shakespeare Theatre and the Manhattan Theatre Club. However, you can be enticed at all levels, depending on your mood and your bank balance. People often say they can't afford to go to the theatre any more because of the cost, with Broadway theatres charging enormous prices, but in London at least there are the stand-by tickets and concession prices usually available.

S N Behrman, a successful American playwright whose plays were as popular in London as in New York, wrote that, "... the one thing that forcibly struck me was the difference between New York and London in what you might call the cultural and social position of the theatre." Backstage in London, he said, the actors' dressing-rooms were where you could meet the most brilliant figures in London society. Lady Sibyl Colefax, accused of being a social snob was defended by Coward: "I think it's quite marvellous that Sibyl fills her house with artists rather than stuffing it with dukes and duchesses." But there were more of the latter stuffing Coward's dressing-room, writes Behrman. (Even today, theatre personalities are accepted by the aristocracy in England.)

A word here about the transatlantic difference in the styles of plays presented: Americans have always shown affection towards and curiosity about the Royal Family, but they don't include them in their plays.

Many of the English comedies are about the English class system, and the tradition of social climbing is as inbred as that of afternoon tea. The British will always have this subject to write about. Some British writers make it their whole career. Alan Ayckbourn must have written as many comedies as Neil Simon, but their subject-matter differs significantly - one could say that Alan deals with the British class system and how it affects their domestic life, whereas Simon deals with totally different characters and uses American humour. The British definitely have hang-ups about class distinctions and their individual places in the class structure; the only subjects remotely equivalent in the United States are the Democratic and Republican political parties, and the mild psychological tensions between Gentiles and Jews.

The new playwrights are more adventurous, and are opening up new themes that are interesting but perhaps less entertaining.

Maugham, Coward, Rattigan have been criticised as being outdated and their plays are no longer regarded as being relevant, just old-fashioned, period pieces to be brought out every so often. However, their plays never offended with their language or characters. One wonders if in the new century, we will have playwrights who, besides being entertaining, will lift our spirits with their wit and elegance. Ever since the angry young men and kitchen sink drama emerged in the mid-fifties we have subjected to a bunch of characters who we sometimes wonder would have been better left in the drawer. Young playwrights will still move us but it will be astonishing if we ever regain some of the old elegance of language and plots that were just such sheer delight. Is it true that the audiences will no longer attend plays that are embarrassing, boring and downright coarse?

Peter Cook said on the subject of plays that he goes to the theatre to be entertained; rape, sodomy, drug addiction he can get at home.

Professional people with disposable income who lead hectic, stressful lives during the day often want to go to the theatre to relax. They want to see stimulating plays, but, nevertheless, most of them don't want to be subjected to the *sturm und drang* of the seamier sides of life - they have enough of that during the day. The plots of operas, for example, are full of tragedy and conflict, but then there is the glorious music to carry them along. Plays need to have a level of inspiration as well, not send the audience out in a worse mood than when they came in. Great acting achieves this, so do great plays. Appreciation of Shakespeare should be taught in all schools so that students can enjoy the plays throughout their lives. Being taught to appreciate the language is essential. Broadway audiences expect all this - hence the popularity of Neil Simon's plays and, before him, Jean Kerr and others.

The differences between London West End and New York theatre are, in spite of superficial similarities, enormous, in a way not dissimilar from the comment about two nations separated by a common language. Even when the same shows are produced in both cities, unless the entire cast is the same, the result will be different. The audiences do not like the same things, they do not laugh at the same jokes, so shows can succeed on Broadway and flop on the West End, and vice-versa.

Broadway and the West End have, with some justification, been seen as rival focal points for world theatre. Each side has its supporters for the claim to being the most vibrant, influential or exciting stretch of theatreland in the world. Broadway's claim rests partly on the fact that, to Americans, it seem inconceivable that little old England should be able to rival, let alone outshine, the vast number of Broadway, Off Broadway and Off-Off Broadway theatres that are one of the many great achievements of the city of New York.

New York itself is so lively, so bustling, so dramatic, that one feels there cannot be anywhere larger or more vibrant than the Big Apple. But the reason stems partly from the often-stated feeling that when you arrive in Manhattan (after all, Manhattan is New York for most visitors despite the splendours and charms that Brooklyn, for example, has to offer) you seem to be on one vast film set. The city is so familiar, thanks to endless films and television series, usually featuring cops and robbers, explosions and wailing sirens. The constant background of hooting horns and the often terrifying speed with which the taxi drivers hurl their cabs through the traffic in order to make sure that you get to the theatre before the curtain goes up, reinforce this feeling of déja-vu, that you have been here before, on the small or silver screen.

The screen is the crucial word, for America is essentially a movie, while England is a play - or musical, perhaps - but a stage one, whatever its form. For all that Broadway has to offer, and despite several decades of effortlessly dominating musical theatre, as an art form, from the 1920s to the 1970s, it remains a junior relation, with all the (friendly) rivalry that goes with family connections, of the West End.

31

And so, if New York is a film set, then London is a stage set. The pageantry that the English perform better than anyone else in the world is a living, everyday reality. London has its famous black cabs (and red buses), but unlike New York's yellow chariots, these symbols of twentieth century speed and convenience have to slow down and make way for the stately pace of horses, when the Household Cavalry makes its way from its barracks in Knightsbridge to the Queen's residence, Buckingham Palace.

The continued, and highly popular, existence of a full-blown monarchy with all the trimmings, lends an extraordinary relevance, and acts as a mirror to, performances of Shakespeare's plays, whether in the great subsidised houses like the National Theatre, or at the Globe, reconstructed a few feet from its original site on the South Bank of the Thames, just yards away from the ancient house where Sir Christopher Wren stayed whilst building St Paul's Cathedral which stands almost opposite, on the north shore of the river.

Yet, for all this, the productions of Shakespeare are modern and innovative, and both the National Theatre and the Royal Shakespeare Company perform, in London, in vast modern (1970s) theatres. True, Shakespeare is also performed in ancient playhouses and the palatial surroundings of Shaftesbury Avenue - an indication of just how large, and varied, London's theatre really is. And, as if it had not been diverse enough, along, in the late 1990s, came the reconstructed Globe Theatre, proving both the health of London's theatrical life and the inter-relation between it and Broadway - or, at least, the United States. For the Globe was re-created thanks to the passion for theatre, the commitment and the courage of an American film director and actor, Sam Wanamaker, who was appalled that Londoners had done nothing to recreate one of the most famous, and influential, theatres in history, Shakespeare's famous "Wooden O".

And, if the superbly built little theatre is a lasting physical testament to the mutual love affair between the American and English acting community, then so, in a more transitory but just as important way, is the presence of American actors on the English stage - the Best of Broadway (and Hollywood) in the heart of the West End.

Dustin Hoffman, for example, was a memorable Shylock in *The Merchant of Venice* at the Theatre Royal, Haymarket, back in the 1980s. He was typical of American actors who feel that they are, in a sense, returning to their roots (or that of their profession, at any rate), and are also in some sense proving themselves as actors, by appearing in a London theatre. If actors are climbers, then, however exciting the other mountain ranges, from New York to Los Angeles or San Francisco, London is definitely their Mount Olympus.

It is true to say that British actors love travelling to New York, too, but this is because a Broadway run looks good on their resumés, and shows that they have been in a commercial success. It is also because America is seen as fun, exciting, different yet strangely familiar, thanks to all those films and TV shows. A spell on Broadway is, therefore, fun and financially rewarding, but it is not seen as an artistic achievement in the same way that a successful and critically acclaimed performance in the West End is seen by American actors.

It is not just actors who admire the West End, however. It is seen, these days, as the ideal venue for playwrights. Arthur Miller, the towering genius and grand old man of the American stage, prefers to preview his plays in the West End, as Broadway has been taken over by large scale musicals, and straight plays are all too rare these days. Managements will rarely wish to risk the large sums involved in putting on a show for a new play, however distinguished the playwright. In London the musical has far less of the stranglehold on mainstream theatres. This is partly a cultural thing - the English love musicals like anyone else, but they have been brought up, for hundreds of years, on well-made plays, and they remain very fond of them, whether they are classic dramas by Sir Terence Rattigan, comedies by Joe Orton or Sir Alan Ayckbourn, or new, controversial plays such as those staged by the famously avant-garde Royal Court Theatre.

After all, the classics, from *King Lear* to *The Duchess of Malfi*, can be terribly violent, but they are well written and the language, however ghastly the deeds it describes and the emotion it conveys, is nonetheless powerful, striking, and beautiful. It would make a pleasant change for young playwrights on both sides of the Atlantic to realise that the more ghastly the action the more carefully crafted the language needs to be. A string of words beginning with "F" doesn't "shock" audiences - it alienates them.

This use of bad language is not, of course, an issue with Arthur Miller, nor with Edward Albee, another Broadway writer whose work has been frequently seen in London in recent years, In particular, his *Three Tall Women* at the exquisite Wyndhams Theatre, and starring Dame Maggie Smith, was a huge success. Her co-star was Frances De La Tour, an actress best known for comic roles, both on stage and on British television, where she was well-known for her role as a female lodger in the long-running 1970s sitcom, *Rising Damp*.

Maggie Smith returned to the West End with another Albee revival, *A Delicate Balance*, at the Theatre Royal Haymarket, one of London's oldest and most attractive theatres, whose name recalls the days when a Royal licence was required to run a playhouse. This time Maggie Smith's co-star was Eileen Atkins, a great actress who is one of the fortunate few actors who is rarely out of work. She had barely finished appearing in *A Delicate Balance* when she began acting, opposite Sir Michael Gambon, in *The Unexpected Man*, a two-hander written by Yasmina Reza, a fashionable French playwright whose clever piece about modern art and the nature of friendship, *Art*, has had a long run at Wyndhams Theatre.

It is not only revivals that make it across the Atlantic, of course. *Angels in America*, which deals with the impact of AIDS, was well received at the National Theatre, while the phenomenally successful rock musical, *Rent*, which updates Puccini's *La Bohème* to the Lower East Side, and replaces the nineteenth century scourge of TB with the twentieth century plague of AIDS, has also been very well received. The Barbican Centre, the vast arts complex in the City of London, that peculiar city-state at the heart of London, with its ancient customs and rights, hosted a year-long celebration of American culture through 1998.

In many ways this celebration was typical of the unique and mutually beneficial relationship between the two countries. Since the Revolution, and with the unfortunate exception of a British invasion that led to the burning of the White House in 1812, the two nations have been close allies, partners in a special relationship that was at its height when powerful, charismatic figures led each country simultaneously - Roosevelt and Churchill, Reagan and Thatcher.

Given this, and given the crucial fact that America, having been founded by the British, speaks English, it is not surprising that the artistic communities of both countries should be so close. That is not to say that the two styles do not sometimes clash. One of the famous of these clashes was that between Laurence Olivier and Marilyn Monroe. Then married to Arthur Miller, she came to London to make *The Prince and the Showgirl*.

This had been performed by Olivier on stage, with his wife, Vivien Leigh, who was replaced in the film version by the younger - and bigger box office - Marilyn. Not a good start: Monroe's way of working was the complete opposite to that of Olivier, and her lateness and, in his opinion, haphazard approach to work used to infuriate him. Despite this, of course, the camera loved her, and she shone through every scene. Olivier, great actor though he undoubtedly was, was also a notoriously jealous performer, so the fact that, despite everything, his co-star easily outshone him on the rushes at the end of every day's shooting used to infuriate him too!

Life has a way of punishing one for one's mistakes or errors of judgement, and Olivier was famously at the receiving end of an almost manic professionalism years later, when he made *Marathon Man* with

Dustin Hoffman, who more or less worked the then elderly Olivier into the ground!

Hoffman, as already mentioned, appeared on the London stage some years later, and many other film stars have taken the same route across the Atlantic. There is little backstage glamour to attract them - theatre dressing-rooms are notoriously shabby and run down, and nothing like the glamorous home-from-homes that movie stars are used to inhabiting between shots on film sets.

It is for this reason that stars have to create a homeliness for themselves, with good-luck cards from fans and admirers, favourite photographs, bouquets of flowers, and the various knickknacks that support and define their stage personalities. Once these are in place, and their dressers have made the rooms a comfortable as possible, they begin to feel at home, and can prepare for, and recover from, their performances.

Dressing-rooms become mini salons in some people's hands, as S N Behrman, the playwright who was once described as "the American Noel Coward" observed. The more outgoing stars love to receive friends and visitors, unwinding after a show with drink, laughter and conversation. Dame Judi Dench's great success (playing, appropriately, a famous actress) in David Hare's *Amy's View* at the Aldwych (1998), was marked by a stream of famous visitors. Ushered in through the stage door, her guests, a positive who's who of the British acting profession, would be shown up the brief flight of stairs to her dressing-room, dominated by a photograph of her actress daughter, Finty. One of her most distinguished visitors was Sir John Mills, the doyen of the British film industry, who had been discovered by Noel Coward in a revue in the Far East. Arriving in a massive Rolls Royce, wearing an immaculate suit and carrying a silver-topped walking stick, Sir John was the embodiment of old world stardom, possessing an elegance that had been passed down from stars like Sir Gerald du Maurier, Jack Buchanan and Rex Harrison.

Visiting backstage after a success is one thing; after a flop, or if one is in a minority who don't actually like the play, it can be a difficult experience. Alan Bennett, the playwright and actor who made his name in the 1960s with *Beyond the Fringe*, and who wrote the play and then the film of *The Madness of King George*, has famously said that almost anything one says to an actor in his/her dressing-room, however the show has gone, will be misinterpreted. Actors, after all, are notoriously insecure, however extravagant their public persona. The only safe thing to do, according to Bennett, is to say, "Marvellous! Marvellous! Marvellous!"

Bennett himself is notoriously shy. On one occasion, when he was starring in his own series of monologues, *Talking Heads*, at the Comedy

Theatre, the Assistant Manager went round to the dressing-room with a message from Princess Margaret, who had come to see the show. Would he care to join Her Royal Highness and her party for dinner afterwards? Bennett, who was lying on a bed in near darkness, poked his head out from under a blanket and murmured, "Oh, I don't think so," before retreating back into the darkness.

What a contrast to Noel Coward, who would have leapt at the opportunity! Who, too, would have dared offer Coward anything but praise if visiting him in his dressing-room after a first night? Coward, on the other hand, was never backward in coming forward with comments and advice to his fellow thespians, and famously accompanied any criticism with a wagging forefinger. His friend and rival, Ivor Novello, had a charming way of disarming Coward, or, indeed, any visitor whom he suspected of having a tendency to comment on, let alone criticise, his shows. As soon as the visitor was ushered into the dressing-room by one of his numerous staff, Ivor would turn round from the dressing-room table, flash them his famous smile and, before they could open their mouths, he would exclaim, loudly, "Oh Ducky! I knew you'd love it!"

The front of house of West End theatres are fascinating places, and not just because of the splendid architecture. The staff, too, are worth a closer look. Although many of the old style theatre managers have gone to the great foyer in the sky, there are still a few who retain the old world charm of their predecessors. But, for a real touch of old England, one needs to look at, and talk to, the bar ladies - the older the better. They too are a dying breed, but there are still enough to bring a touch of cockney charm to the age-old process of drinking at the bar. Catch them at the right moment and in the right mood, and you will hear stories of how they served Marlene Dietrich, or Charlton Heston, or how they took an afternoon off to watch Lauren Bacall in *Sweet Bird of Youth* at the Haymarket.

Ask any of these older women who the most beautiful actress they have ever seen was, and the reply is almost always the same: Vivien Leigh. The Dress Circle bar at the Aldwych is surrounded by pictures of stars who have graced its stage, and Miss Leigh is there among them, shining out across the years, immortalised in her delicate, and tragic, beauty.

Vivien Leigh is fascinating, not just for her beauty, but for the way that her career echoes the remarkable links between England and America, Broadway and the West End. An English Rose, a product of the British Empire (her father worked in India, and the young Vivien was sent "home" to England for her education), an actress who, as Lady Olivier, was one half of the most glamorous couple in theatre history (with apologies to

Joan Crawford and Douglas Fairbanks Junior), she was a great Shakespearean actress who toured the world in some of his most demanding roles. And yet, Miss Leigh's greatest successes were to the British, on stage, yet, just as memorably, on film to the Americans.

Her greatest claim to fame, which will earn her immortality as long as people ever watch films, was as Scarlett O'Hara, the star - and villain - of *Gone With the Wind*. This film's enduring popularity was beautifully demonstrated by the advertisement on the frontage of the Odeon cinema in London's Leicester Square at the time the *Titanic* opened there. It quoted a critic saying that *Titanic* was this generation's *Gone With The Wind*!

A glance at both the London and New York magazines will reveal a remarkable cross-fertilisation of talent (not to mention the audience). The West End relies heavily on American tourists to swell the box office receipts, especially in the summer, when most resident Londoners try to escape the city for British beaches or foreign resorts. In the summer of 1998 one of the most sought-after tickets was for *The Iceman Cometh*, transferred from the Almeida Theatre, Islington (in effect an Off Broadway playhouse) to the Old Vic. However marvellous the play, the direction, and the rest of the cast, the main attraction was clearly the dominating presence of Kevin Spacey, the film actor.

Across the "pond", New York played host to a tour by the prestigious Royal Shakespeare Company, to Richard Briers and Geraldine McEwan in a new play, transferred from the Royal Court, and the young British actor, Alan Cumming, was earning acclaim as the MC in *Cabaret*, in a production that had moved to Broadway from the Donmar Warehouse, the beautifully converted theatre space in the heart of London's Covent Garden.

Americans who go to the theatre in London are often surprised that they have to pay for their programmes - usually either £2 or £2.50 each. Although this may seem an unreasonable charge, for those used to receiving them free on Broadway, it should be remembered that one often gets far more editorial and interesting information in the English programmes than in their New York counterparts, and also - and crucially - that the theatre seats cost far less in London. It may seem odd that the centre of London's film area (with a nearby statue of Charlie Chaplin to prove it) has a square, but there is no comparable theatre square, all the main playhouses fronting directly onto the streets. The nearest equivalent might have been St James's Square, but this is almost exclusively taken up by the wonderful gardens, dominated by a statue of King William III. The St James's Theatre, where Oscar Wilde's *The Importance of Being Earnest*, among the most entertaining comedies ever, was just around the corner from the Square (which is faced by the imposing portico of the Theatre Royal Haymarket, though separated from it by two streets) but was pulled down in the late 1950s, despite a vigorous protest led by Vivien Leigh.

American theatre is on the brink of a dramatic change, as important as the establishment of Off Broadway or the onset of television. No longer isolated and distinct from and independent of cinema, television and the recording industry (videos, CDs etc.), theatre is becoming "content" - Disney (*The Lion King*), SFX (*Riverdance, Tap Dogs, Stomp*), so not only no new plays but no new musicals on Broadway, only revivals (*Peter Pan, Annie Get Your Gun*).

The role of Broadway might have been carried on by Off Broadway and even Off-Off Broadway, but they need either public or private sponsorship, and plays first put on there now rarely transfer to Broadway. The Lincoln Center Theatre and two regional theatres are collaborating with the entertainment industry giants on the production of musicals.

The effect of all this on the young and potential theatre audiences must surely be one of "dumbing down". What is being seen in theatres is less and less straight plays; even the musicals which are largely superseding them seem to be giving way to spectacles rather than theatre of any kind, with special effects (as in the cinema too) dominating the theatrical qualities of the performance.

Fringe benefits from the Atlantic alliance

New York theatre relies on the freshness, originality (and cheap tickets!) of Off and Off-Off Broadway for a regular infusion of new talent, from actors and directors to choreographers and lighting designers. London's theatrical health is similarly dependent on new blood from the Fringe - a term that covers everything from tiny theatres above pubs to converted warehouses with all mod cons.

It is fascinating to note that, just as Broadway and the West End demonstrate a remarkable cross-fertilisation of talent, so do the Off and Fringe theatres. Three theatres, each very different in location and style, are linked by this common theme. The Almeida Theatre is in Islington, an essentially eighteenth century area of London, a little to the North of the historic City, and now a very fashionable area - Prime Minister Blair lived there until he moved to Downing Street after winning the 1997 General Election.

The Almeida has succeeded in having an enormous profile for so small a venue by a highly effective policy of inviting leading movie actors from both sides of the Atlantic (Kevin Spacey, Julia Binoche, Ralph Fiennes,

Diana Rigg) to perform for minute salaries. The draw has been the chance to appear in live theatre (not that Dame Diana Rigg is short of such opportunities!) in exciting productions of great classics, both modern and old.

The Donmar Warehouse is, as its name implies, a converted warehouse, and is located in the historic and beautiful Covent Garden area of central London. The contrast between the almost unbroken artistic success of Sam Mendes (the talented young director of the Donmar) and the vicissitudes and office politics of the nearby Royal Opera House is striking - all the more so given the vast sums of public money that the Opera House has traditionally received, and the struggle that the Donmar has had to sustain enough sponsorship to survive.

The Donmar has played hosts to a variety of legendary American stars, one of the most recent being Barbara Cook, who appeared in cabaret there in a series appropriately called *Diva*. She was followed, only a couple of weeks later, by Nicole Kidman, playing opposite Ian Glenn in *The Blue Room*. Nicole Kidman is, of course, a leading movie star with a heady mix of great talent and striking beauty, both of which are enhanced, in the public eye, by the fact that she is Mrs Tom Cruise. This combination (not forgetting Mr Glenn's contribution, of course, or that of writer/translator David Hare) ensured "House Full" signs outside the Donmar almost as soon as the booking period opened!

Repaying the debt that London owes to the Wanamaker family, who have been responsible for the recreation of Shakespeare's Globe Theatre on the south bank of the Thames, the Donmar has also seen Zoe Wanamaker perform in several roles, one of the most striking being in Tennessee Williams' *The Glass Menagerie*. Lest it seem that the Donmar's relationship with America is entirely one way, however, it should be noted that it is a Donmar Warehouse production - of *Cabaret* - that has been the toast of Broadway in 1998. *Cabaret* itself is, of course, a transatlantic creation, being an American musical based on an Englishman's (Christopher Isherwood) experiences in Germany in the 1930s.

The third such theatre is the Bridewell, a converted swimming pool in a large, attractive Victorian building owned by a City of London charity, next door to the historic St Bride's Church (where the parents of Virginia Dare, the first white child born in America) were married. The Victorian swimming pool hall was in use until some twenty or so years ago, but was then boarded over. In its heyday it had always been closed each winter, but the boards were, literally, trod by actors, for the Institute's amateur operatic society used to perform operettas (usually by Gilbert and Sullivan) in the hall.

By the early 1990s these performances belonged to the distant past, but the Governors of the Institute decided to convert the now largely derelict hall (that was used for table-tennis matches) into a theatre-cum-conference space. The first step was a Shakespearean performance given in the unreconstructed hall, with a splash of paint on the walls, air fresheners liberally scattered around the building to dispel the inevitable mustiness to be found in a dilapidated basement!

Under the artistic direction of Carol Metcalfe the swimming pool hall became a successful fringe venue. Its name, the Bridewell Theatre, came from the old Bridewell Palace, a royal residence on the edge of whose site the St Bride Institute stands. The main reception room of the Institute is also named after the Palace, and has a picture of it on its walls.

Ms Metcalfe was particularly interested in musicals, and in Stephen Sondheim's in particular, and she achieved the remarkable feat of persuading him to be the theatre's patron, as well as staging a number of very well received productions of his shows. Perhaps Sondheim simply recognised her talent and drive, but perhaps he was also amused by the fact that the Bridewell Theatre is located just off the eastern end of Fleet Street, the setting for one of his musicals, *Sweeney Todd*. Sweeney Todd, you will remember, was the "demon barber of Fleet Street" several of whose unfortunate customers had their throats cut rather than their hair, and were unceremoniously converted into delicious meat pies!

All three theatres demonstrate, therefore, the way in which the British and Broadway continue to influence each other, with the Atlantic not so much a barrier as a bridge, linking the artistic achievements of both the great English-speaking nations. Churchill would have been proud.

I'm the end of the line. Absurd and appalling as it may seem, serious New York theatre has died in my lifetime.

Arthur Miller, *The Times*, 11th January 1989

CHAPTER FIVE

FOLLOWING IN NOEL COWARD'S FOOTSTEPS

"There will always be a stinging enchantment in this arrival. Even now, when 1 know it so well in every aspect, my heart jumps a little, Then it was entirely new to me." So Coward recalled his first impression of New York in 1921. "We slid gently past Battery Park, still green with early summer. The skyscrapers moved gracefully aside to show still further vistas, and, a long way below us, platoons of straw hats passed by on ferry-boats. As we drew near the dock, several fussy little tugs came out to meet us and finally, after tremendous efforts, succeeded in coaxing and nuzzling us alongside."

If any one Englishman can be said to sum up the English affair with New York, it must surely be Sir Noel Coward.

In many ways, *I Like America* was as much an anthem to his life as *Mad Dogs and Englishmen,* for as a young man Coward was inspired, as were so many of his generation, by the excitement and vitality of America in general, and New York in particular; in middle age he was to find America a refuge and a source of income - the New World coming to the rescue of the Old.

It is easy to forget how, in the 1920s, when Noel Coward began to achieve the fame and fortune that his mother had been so sure was his birthright, America seemed to be a heady mixture of the safe (no ghastly tropical diseases like the profitable but perilous parts of the British Empire that had earned nicknames like "The White Man's Grave") and the exciting - a *Brave New World* that combined democracy with capitalism, that welcomed the huddled masses who yearned to be free, but which exported jazz, affordable motor cars, and a breezy, fresh attitude to life that stood in stark contrast to the shattered societies of a Europe that had been broken by the First World War.

In England, even the Prince of Wales, the inheritor of Empire, the future King and Emperor, took American fashions to heart, and adopted - in rebellion against his father - a half-cockney, half-American accent.

It was not surprising, therefore, that the young Noel Coward decided that he would travel to New York, hoping that he would take the city by storm. His thoughts seemed to be on the lines of the song made famous by Frank Sinatra. If Coward could make it there, people back in

London would have to sit up and take notice. He would, literally, have arrived.

It was with the glamorous image of New York in his mind, and with his name in lights on Broadway as his most heartfelt wish, that Coward travelled, on a Cunard liner (naturally!) across the Atlantic, accompanied by an aristocratic English friend, Jeffrey Amherst, in May 1921.

The *Aquitania* seemed to symbolise the glamorous world that Coward was convinced was his by right, but fate gave him a warning of the trials ahead when many of the ship's crew - including, vitally, the cooks - went on strike! Having survived this example of backstage rebellion, Coward caught his first glimpse of Manhattan on a gorgeous June morning.

Even today, the experience of gliding past the skyscrapers and docks of New York is exciting, however often one may have done it, but to a young man in the early 1920s it must have been breathtaking.

A stickler for doing things well, and aiming for the best, Coward made straight for the Algonquin hotel, but he could barely wait to deliver his suitcases before rushing off to Broadway. For Noel had theatre in the blood - not for nothing was this the author of *The Boy Actor*, a superb and moving poem about a child actor whose formative years were spent, not on the games field, but on stage. Not for him the cheers of his fellows as he scored a goal - his adrenaline surged not to muddy fields but to the smell of greasepaint, the tattered glamour of theatre dressing-rooms, the sound of the front-of-house orchestra, the thrill of an extra curtain call.

Coward's delight in Broadway reflects the fact that, for all the British pride in London's theatreland, even the most patriotic of British actors (and Noel Coward, after all, wrote that love song to the city, *London Pride*, at the height of the Second World War) realised that Broadway was somewhere special. Not just because of the traditions of its stately theatres (many of which were as old as anything London had to offer, after all), but because of the sheer electricity in the air (and on the billboards!), the use of the latest marketing techniques to make the desirable seem unmissable.

The excitement that was a hallmark of Broadway was also reflected in the hectic social life of the city, particularly among the rather more adventurous, theatrical set. Coward made many new friends as well as bumping into chums from London who, like him, had come to America in search of dollars. This change from the Edwardian procedure - when rich American girls would come to England in search of titles and all the grander appurtenances of "class" - marked the huge sea-change that the First World War had created. Although Britain had won the war, and survived the revolutions that swept the continent, it was already clear, to those with foresight, that this was to be the American century.

During this first stay in New York, Noel's fortunes proved to be more evasive than he had expected, and his accommodation, which had started so grandly at the Algonquin, moved progressively downwards into ever more humble circumstances. He was given a lifeline by Gabrielle Enthoven, a theatre enthusiast who left a vast collection of theatre memorabilia to the Theatre Museum, Covent Garden.

While trying to break into Broadway, Noel met two vitally important friends, Alfred Lunt and Lynn Fontanne, for whom he wrote, and with whom he co-starred in *Design For Living* some years later, when all three were safely successful. The play has been sporadically revived since the 1930s, but is primarily of interest for its biographical background rather than its artistic merit - in the 1995 revival at the Globe Theatre (now renamed the Gielgud, in honour of Sir John Gielgud) it was hard to really care for any of the three characters, and their bisexual love tangle was not so much daring as rather passé.

While the acting work was in abeyance, Noel wrote stories which he was able to sell, including to *Vanity Fair*. This provided him with periodic bursts of income, but he had to cut his cloth according to his means, so instead of the lavish lunches that he was to so greatly enjoy once he became a success, he dined, in less than splendour, at an Italian deli in McDougal Street. When eating at home, bereft of air-conditioning and in the full blast of a New York summer, he prepared his food stark naked, unaware that his anatomy was easily viewed by passers-by and neighbours. In one of those famous incidents that swiftly became part of Noel Coward folklore, he was called on by a bad-tempered policeman, whose indignation was quickly overcome - despite the obvious disadvantage - by Noel's extraordinary charm. Aided, one suspects, by the fact that the charm was accompanied by half a bottle of wine, the policeman not only left Noel to his own devices, but gave him his revolver, as the neighbourhood was notoriously dangerous. It makes a great story, but one can't help thinking that the likelihood of a hardened precinct cop handing over his revolver to a strange, naked Englishman, let alone leaving it at his apartment, beggars belief. Mind you, quite a lot of Coward's career was distinctly larger than life …

Another larger-than-life Englishman who was in New York at the time, and whom Coward met up with, was Ronald Colman, who was soon to have the most famous little moustache since Charlie Chaplin, but who at the time was as much a penniless hopeful as Coward himself. Noel got over the lack of money as he did all obstacles - with charm and determination. Accounts of his time in New York, therefore, alternate between accounts of poverty (having to borrow money from Lynn

Fontanne, for example) and descriptions of society parties on the Upper East Side, and country house parties, at least one of which was thought to be the origin for *Hay Fever*, one of his most successful comedies. When he left for England, as the leaves began to fall in Central Park, Noel Coward had failed to make the professional breakthrough that he had anticipated, but had launched himself on the social scene, and was confident - and determined - that he would return.

The fact that he did return, throughout his career, was evidence of the two-way love affair between Coward and New York. On his second visit, in 1924, his songs were performed in André Charlot's *Revue of 1924* - a show that may not have had a very exciting title(though a starry cast that included Jack Buchanan and Gertrude Lawrence), but became a hit as the Charlot Revues caught the mood of the age. It is easy, at this distance, to forget that memories of the First World War were still very much in people's minds. The hedonism of the 1920s was a reaction to the horrors of the war and this was a period when the well-to-do had the resources to live well and dine late. Revues were the perfect entertainment for smart New York (and London) society - clever and amusing yet easily digestible. Pictures taken at the time show the audiences to have been beautifully and formally dressed, determined to have a glamorous night out. They would have been astonished had they seen the dressing down that generally takes place today, particularly in London. New York audiences, by and large, are much better dressed than West End ones.

During his 1924 stay, Noel began at the Ritz Hotel, on Madison Avenue, but decided to economise by moving to a friend's flat on East 32nd Street. When he returned to the city in 1926 he again started out at the Ritz, but swiftly decided that the place was too expensive, so moved to the Gladstone on East 52nd Street - a smart but simpler base from which to operate.

He was in New York for the opening of his play, *This Was a Man*, but the rehearsals went so badly (as was often the case with his productions) that he decamped to Long Island. When the play opened on 22nd November it was a failure. The old theatrical adage that a disastrous dress rehearsal meant a successful first night was not proved true on this occasion. Coward quipped to a friend that the actors' delivery of his script was so ploddingly slow that there was time to pop out and get an ice cream between each line!

Noel's next visit, in 1928 was a reconnaissance mission rather than a production, but he took the opportunity, during his two week stay, to catch up with all the latest shows. On arrival he checked into the Ritz (of course!) and gave a press interview, in which he claimed that he felt perfectly at home in New York, whose theatre-going public were much friendlier and more enthusiastic than whose in London. Even allowing for a little judicious buttering-up of the local newspapers, Noel had put his finger on a truth that still holds good - Americans enjoy and applaud success, while the English are extremely wary of it. The English sympathy in invariably with the plucky underdog rather than the triumphant winner, and they don't really give themselves over to stars until those stars are old and safely past their prime; then it is considered good form to admire them. A classic example of this is Dame Gracie Fields, who had plenty of problems during her prime, particularly during the Second World War when she was married to an Italian citizen; yet she was trundled out on stage to tumultuous applause and genuine affection when she was an old lady.

The frenetic pace, the flaunting of wealth, the sense of fun, that characterised the New York of the 1920s was shattered by the Wall Street Crash in 1929. The knock-on effect reverberated around the world, and were reflected in the theatre as well as other spheres of life. Noel was still writing comedies (most notably, of course, *Private Lives*), but there was an added depth and maturity to his work, as well as a sense of nostalgia and foreboding. *Cavalcade* was patriotic tribute to the past, but also a warning about the future, a suggestion that there might be another - disaster (there is a scene on board the doomed liner in the show) looming ahead.

Atlantic liners continued to convey Noel safely over the waves, however, and he chose to commemorate this international lifestyle by naming a production company, set up in the early 30s, "Trans-Atlantic Presentations". Realising the good sense of owning his own place in New York he bought an apartment on East 52nd Street, but his stay there (in 1936) was brief, as he suffered one of his periodic nervous breakdowns. These were a characteristic of his career, and were, in a sense, a safety valve. He was so full of ideas, of energy, and of a ruthless determination to succeed, that he lived life at a pace and intensity far greater than most of his contemporaries - which is, perhaps, why we remember him while they are long since forgotten.

It was to recover from these personal crises that he travelled abroad so often and in the luxurious and relaxing manner of luxury ocean liners. Given that he divided his career between two of the greatest cities on earth, and given the phenomenal pace of life in New York, which was then, and still remains, the most exciting and vibrant metropolis on the planet, it is little wonder that these much needed holidays occurred so frequently.

When the world hit its equivalent of a collective breakdown, with the outbreak of the Second World War, Noel sailed to New York in order to arouse sympathy and support for Britain. He left for America in April 1940, shortly before the invasion and fall of France that was to leave Britain to face Nazi Europe alone. Officially, he was there to promote a new play (after all, the United States was a neutral country at the time) but the reality was that he was to be a one-man propaganda mission for England (rather as his friend and fellow composer/playwright, Ivor Novello, had been sent to Stockholm, in neutral Sweden, during the First World War). The fact that he was able to enjoy un-rationed food and a pre-war lifestyle in New York which was now just a memory in London, was an added attraction.

The war years saw Noel working in England and touring the Empire, with morale-boosting concerts for the troops. Once the war had been safely won, however, he returned to America, but *his Tonight at 8.30* was not the success he had hoped for. The late 1940s and the 1950s were a very low period for Coward. Tastes had changed - the world had changed - and in many ways he seemed dated and out of touch. His big post-war musical, *Pacific 1860*, starring Mary Martin, was a flop. What could he do? As the 1950s wore on, he had the added problem of income tax problems - the Labour government that had been elected by a landslide in 1945 had put taxes up to pay for a socialist transformation of the country. Noel was an unashamed conservative, and was appalled by both government politics as well as its economics, but it was the latter that hit the hardest.

What was he to do? At a time when America was at the height of its economic boom, it seemed that it might, as it had thirty years earlier, be a launching pad for his career. The growth of television (which was still relatively rare in England - it took the Queen's coronation in 1953 to kick-start it as a popular pastime in the United Kingdom) seemed to offer a solution, and Noel took the opportunity with both hands. He may have grown older and statelier, but at heart he was still the ambitious, determined man who had climbed from lower-middle-class obscurity to international fame and fortune.

Most of the money that Noel made in America came from appearing in cabaret in Las Vegas, and there is a famous record cover picture showing him standing, dressed in a tuxedo, in the Nevada Desert. The idea for this work came from his having introduced Marlene Dietrich at the Cafe de Paris in London. If a huge star like her could, after the war, re-invent herself as a cabaret star, representing pre-war glamour and style, then so, in his way, could he.

In addition to Las Vegas cabaret, however, he also appeared on New York television, for CBS. And it was in New York that he met Mike Todd, the producer - and husband of Elizabeth Taylor. Todd persuaded him to take a part in *Around the World in Eighty Days* which starred David Niven, another Englishman famed for his old world glamour and gentlemanly disposition. This was, sadly, to be Todd's only film, as he was killed in a plane crash not long after.

During the production of the TV show, Noel stayed in an apartment on East 54th Street - it had taken twenty years to move two streets further towards the Upper East Side!! The show, called *Together With Music* was a great success, even though (or perhaps because) he had smoothed away some of the sexier lines in some of his songs, in deference to the rather more puritanical nature of American television audiences.

Tax troubles had led to Noel's working in America, and he decided to become a tax exile, as he had no intention of leading an impoverished old age. Much as he loved America, it was not the best place for him to live for this reason, so he bought homes in Bermuda (of which he tired) and then Switzerland, as well as his beloved Firefly, in Jamaica. It was while en route to Jamaica that he made his last ever journey to New York, in January 1973, to see a production of *Oh Coward*.

Fittingly, he made his final public appearance there, with his old friend Marlene Dietrich. After a week's residence in New York he travelled on to Jamaica, where he died, two months later.

One of the best recordings available of Noel Coward performing his work, is a CD called *The Noel Coward Album*. Suitably, it is made up of recordings taken during performances in the States, in Las Vegas and in his beloved New York. His attitude to the States was summed up in the song, *I Like America*, but his love of New York could best be described, I feel, in the words of one of his comedy numbers: "I Went to a Marvellous Party". Noel may have died, but if his spirit lives on, one of the places at which it is to be found is surely at an after-theatre party in the heart of Manhattan.

Men go to the theatre to forget; women, to remember. In the theatre, a hero is one who believes that all women are ladies, a villain, one who believes all ladies are women.

George Jean Nathan, *The Theatre*

Chapter Six

Ivor Novello and the British Musical

There has been a considerable revival of interest, in recent years, in the life and career of Ivor Novello, the composer of a string of classic British movies, plays and revues. Although I am a great fan of the better-known Noel Coward, I have found, since my visit to Novello's flat next to the Waldorf Hotel in London's West End, that I have been drawn to Novello - or "Ivor" as he was known to his friends and fans.

At first sight there does not seem to be much of a link between Novello and New York. He died, aged 58, in 1951, so he didn't have the same opportunities for television appearances as his friend and friendly rival, Noel Coward. Noel was able to redefine his public image in the 1950s through East Coast television specials and through regular and highly paid cabaret appearances in Las Vegas. Ivor had achieved considerable success in London during and immediately after the First World War through a string of late-night revues at fashionable theatres, and his facility for a catchy tune would have ensured success had he lived long enough to follow Noel's example.

Noel's cabaret shows were inspired by those of his old friend, Marlene Dietrich, and Ivor was also a friends of hers; he befriended other Hollywood stars whom he had met during his year or so in Hollywood in the early 1930s, when an otherwise barren period was enlivened by his work on the script of the first Tarzan film, *Tarzan the Ape Man*, starring John Weissemuller.

Ivor Novello is primarily known for his musicals, which made him the most popular and prolific composer of British musicals until Andrew (now Lord) Lloyd Webber began his meteoric rise to fame in the 1970s. Ivor's shows are generally described as "Ruritanian" and are, in a sense, operettas, drawing on the great romantic tradition (and the often overlooked comedy) of the Viennese masters like Franz Lehar, whose greatest work, *The Merry Widow*, was seen by the young Ivor Novello twenty-seven times!

These musicals of Ivor's, which earned him a fortune in England (he had a London penthouse, a country mansion, and a house in Jamaica, a Rolls Royce, and numerous servants as well as an army of secretaries, helpers and awe-struck camp followers) never transferred to Broadway.

Yet despite this, it is the case that there were very strong links between Ivor and New York, and the American theatre and cinema were important influences on his career.

New York first made an impact on him as a teenager, when he travelled to North America (Canada and the States) with his mother, Clara Novello Davies. This formidable woman was small, round, and with a fiery Welsh temperament and a talent that was propelled - and sometimes damaged - by her enormous determination to succeed. This talent was passed on to her son, who displayed it in a far less blatant way, and as soon as she was able to assure herself that her only child was indeed the musical prodigy that he had prayed for, she groomed him to be a great composer.

Even when Ivor was at the top of his profession, a film star, playwright, actor and composer of smash hit musicals, she insisted on carrying on with her own career as a choirmistress and singing teacher. It was in the first capacity that she took Ivor to the States in 1911, where he caught the New World love of modernity that was also to win over the young Prince of Wales, later Edward VIII.

It was in the second capacity that she took a studio in New York for six months of the year, having been as impressed by the size, splendour and vitality of New York as her impressionable and theatre-mad son. Clara Novello Davies was not a woman to let anything as inartistic as a war get in way, so even when the German U-boats (that were to sink the *Lusitania* and bring the United States, reluctantly, into the First World War) threatened civilian shipping in the Atlantic sea-lanes, she insisted on crossing the "pond" to bring her unique - and highly effective - singing and breath-control methods to a willing, well-moneyed clientele of New York ladies.

By and large Clara fitted into New York society very well, though her deliberate flouting of conventions by inviting blacks (albeit statuesque and talented ones who would have been an adornment to any event) to her lavish parties did not go down terribly well with many of her neighbours. Party-giving was in her blood, so the money she made from her fashionable lessons was always eaten up by the time her "season" ended, so she was compelled, for financial reasons as much as artistic or career ones, to return each following year.

If Ivor Novello's first experience of New York was as a good looking appendage to his mother's entourage, his next extended visit was as a strikingly handsome film star and successful actor and playwright - in short, a star. Having become rich and famous at the age of twenty-one, in 1914, by composing the extraordinarily poignant and popular anthem to a lost generation of war-battered soldiers, *Keep The Home Fires Burning*, he went on to write music for revues, as already mentioned, and then, in 1919, the year after the War finally dragged to a close (before beginning a re-run, in 1939) he became a movie star.

Louis Mercanton, the French film director, spotted Ivor's photo in an agent's file, and although he was there as a composer, his Italianate dark good looks, and the soon-to-be-famous profile clinched the deal for Mercanton, who cast him as the lead in *L'Appel du Sang*, a torrid melodrama about a young man (Ivor) who falls in love with a Sicilian girl and is murdered by a jealous relative.

This early success was followed up with *The White Rose*, directed by the great D W Griffith, who was already past his creative prime, but still a name to conjure with. The story goes that Griffith, when in London, used to dine at the Savoy, one of London's most prestigious, and exclusive restaurants (as Paul Robeson was to find - he was allowed to appear on stage in *Othello* at the neighbouring Savoy Theatre, but not permitted to dine at the hotel). Ivor, knowing that the great man was in town and looking for a leading man for his next film, made sure he had a table near the director's, and made equally sure that Griffith caught the full force of his devastating good looks, especially the Novello profile. As Noel Coward was to later quip, "There are two perfect things in this world - my brain and Ivor's profile."

Having succeeded in catching Griffith's attention, Ivor was cast in *The White Rose*, and went on from there to star in a variety of British silent movies, including Alfred Hitchcock's first success, *The Lodger* (1926). He combined this film career with the life of an actor and playwright (which ensured he got the lead roles that suited him most!), and so, when he arrived by liner at New York in 1930, the American public was used to seeing photos and reading gossip about him in film magazines and the popular press.

Interest in the British visitor, who came to Broadway to appear in *Symphony in Two Flats*, a play that was equally divided between comedy and tragedy, was heightened by the fact that Ivor was rumoured to be in love with fellow passenger, Gladys Cooper (grandmother of the theatre historian, critic, and Playbill writer, Sheridan Morley). Ivor and Gladys were indeed very close, and had co-starred in a silent movie about the life of *Bonnie Prince Charlie* (1923), but both their hearts were otherwise engaged, and they were, to use the classic phrase, just good friends.

The summer of 1930 was not the ideal time to arrive on Broadway with a foreign play. Quite apart from the seasonal warm weather, which in pre-air-conditioning days made play-going an uncomfortable business (as American visitors to London still find all too often!), *Symphony in Two*

12 *Above Uncle Vanya*, 1945 - Ralph Richardson as Vanya, Laurence Olivier as Astrov.
13 *Below* Backstage with John Springer alongside Elizabeth Taylor and Richard Burton.

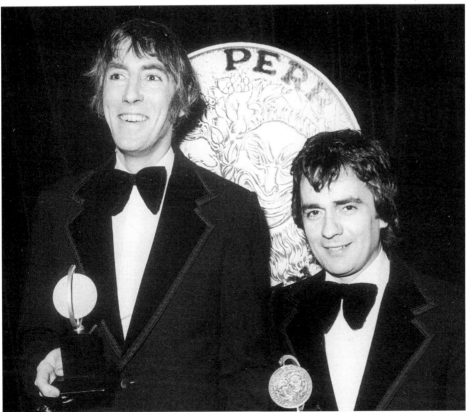

14 *Above left*
Robert Morley
in *Edward My
Son.*
15 *Above right*
Noel Coward
and Gertrude
Lawrence in
Private Lives,
1930.
16 *Below* Peter
Cooke and
Dudley Moore
accepting the
Tony Award in
New York.

17 *Above left* Roundabout Theatre - one of three famous Broadway theatres which have housed British hits from the West End with British stars and British playwrights.
18 *Above right* Statue of Sir Noel Coward, unveiled on 1st March 1999 at the Gershwin.
19 *Below* The Brooks Atkinson Theatre.

20 *Far left* The British invasion continues—1999—Judi Dench at the Ethel Barrymore Theatre in *Amy's View* by David Hare.

21 *Right* Natasha Richardson stars in *Closer*. The play transferred from the West End.

22 *Below* Shakespeare and Co Bookshop, Lexington Avenue near Hunter Avenue.

23 *Left* George M Cohan's statue in Times Square.
24 *Above* Actors' Equity Offices - 165 West 46th Street, only forty-five steps from Broadway.
25 *Below* Lyceum Theatre - built in 1903 by Daniel Frohman. His apartment above the theatre houses the Shubert Archives. Still visible is the famous peep-hole where he could watch his actress wife, famous Margaret Illington, on stage. John Osborne's *Look Back in Anger* played here when it was transferred from London.

26 *Above left* The Lambs Club was built by the architect Standford White. This shows the original location which is now a church. The Lambs have moved to the Women's Republican Club on West 51st Street. Many portraits and posters of former Lambs' members can be seen in their private rooms there. The artist who painted the murals at the Cafe des Artistes, Howard Chandler Christy, also painted posters for the Lambs' events.
27 *Above right* Portrait of Edwin Booth by John S Sargent, at the Players.
28 *Below* Bea Lillie, also at the Players.

29 *Above left* The Players' front door
at 16 Gramercy Park.
30 *Above right* Top floor at Players
showing Booth's study and
bedroom.
31 *Below right* Michael Allinson - a
British actor who has played on
Broadway many times; he is also
the President of the Players' Club.

32 *Above* Famous actors are featured in the lobby at the Players.
33 *Below left* The bust of Sir John Gielgud at the Players Club.
34 *Below right* A plaque of Henry Irving at the Players.

Flats was not Ivor's most brilliant play. The other factor in this commercial equation was that the Wall Street Crash of Fall 1929 was less that a year away, and the financial repercussions were still being felt by a great many people. Regular theatre-goers were an endangered species!

The play was put on by that great theatre dynasty, the Shuberts, and taken off again soon after. Ivor's determination to succeed, nurtured by his mother and re-enforced by a decade of stardom, meant that he was not about to turn tail and head back for London. Although his mother's glory days as the diva teacher of New York were now over, it was inconceivable to him to be defeated by a city he admired and loved, and which his mother had, in her own way, conquered. He appealed to the Shuberts to try with a more commercial play of his, and they had the good sense to agree.

The Truth Game was one of the inter-war drawing-room comedies in which Ivor excelled, and which have been almost completely forgotten, over-shadowed as they were by his later achievements in the field of musical theatre. It may well be that his musicals would be too expensive to recreate on stage today (though given the cost of so many Broadway hits, it shouldn't be impossible), but couldn't a producer at least try with one of his plays? After all, Noel Coward's early work was either forgotten or discredited when Sir Laurence Olivier had the guts to stage *Hay Fever*, a light comedy dating from the 1920s, at the National Theatre in 1964.

The Truth Game was staged at the Ethel Barrymore Theatre, and co-starred Billie Burke, the wife of the legendary showman, Florenz Ziegfeld, who threw a huge party for Ivor at his Hudson River home. Given this combination of acting talent, and the strength of the play's script, it is not surprising that the show was a hit with critics and public alike. During the run of *The Truth Game* Ivor became very friendly with a wealthy young American, Richard Rose, who was later to co-produce several of his shows in England. It was Rose who found Ivor a new flat after Bea Lillie, in whose home Ivor had originally stayed, returned to New York from London.

In his fascinating memoir of his association with Ivor, *Perchance to Dream*, Mr Rose describes how he concocted a bathtub full of illicit gin (this was during Prohibition, of course). The party clearly went with a swing, and Ivor's life-long ability to attract the brightest lights in the theatre and film world meant that the first-night party was described as "The Party of the Stars".

It was this prolonged experience of New York, together with his more general admiration for American talent, that led to Ivor's habit of casting American leading ladies in his very British (or, at least, given the operetta background, European) musicals. Before discussing them it might be helpful just to list the best of them: *Glamorous Night* (1935) *Careless Rapture* (1936), *Crest of the Wave* (1937), *The Dancing Years* (1939), *Perchance to Dream* (1945), *King's Rhapsody* (1949). He also wrote *Arc de Triomphe* (1943) and *Gay's The Word* (1951).

Of these musicals, only *Glamorous Night* and *King's Rhapsody* could really be described as Ruritanian, in the sense of being set in make-believe European kingdoms. *The Dancing Years* was set in Vienna, over a period of some twenty-five years, *Perchance to Dream* was set in an English house over several generations, while *Careless Rapture* and *Crest of the Wave* involve globe-trotting changes of scenery that resemble nothing so much as a James Bond movie, in their blend of action, comedy, and exotic locations.

And that, really, was one of the major factors in Ivor's consistent run of success - he provided entertainment, plus some much-needed glamour, in a way that was matched only by the lavish Hollywood musicals.

Given that "American" meant glamour, excitement and modernity to inter-war Britain, it is not, in retrospect, surprising that Ivor chose American leading women to launch his series of musicals. This fact has, however, been glossed over by many people, and is not known to the general public in Britain today - they would be surprised to learn that so many of his leading ladies came from the States. To be fair, this is partly because they all seem to have fallen in love with England (and, one suspects, with Ivor!) and settled in London for the rest of their lives. Mary Ellis, the first of his leading ladies, still lives there, at the time of writing (1998), in a beautiful flat in Eaton Square, just opposite where the beautiful but tragic Vivien Leigh lived and, in 1967, died.

Mary Ellis had begun as a singer at the New York Met, moved into commercial musical theatre (*Rose Marie*) and then into "straight" theatre, a genre to which she was to return in later life after her exquisite voice, which we are fortunate enough to be able to enjoy on CDs of her classic recordings, finally gave up on her. Her last musical was for Noel Coward, in *After the Ball*, his musical version of Oscar Wilde's *Lady Windemere's Fan*. The experience was not a great success, for Mary Ellis or for the show, and just proves that Ivor (and his ladies) and Noel didn't really mix on stage. Coward's greatest flop had been a show, *Sirocco*, that starred a reluctant Ivor Novello, in London in 1927. For years afterwards, if a show bombed on its first night, actors would merely have to mutter the word *Sirocco* as a shorthand that would explain the full extent of the failure to their fellow professionals.

Mary's experience with Ivor, however, was entirely happy, at least in the big shows (*Arc de Triomphe* was one of his rare failures). He chose her because she was that rare combination of a beauty, a superb singer, and a remarkably gifted actress. His next leading lady, in both *Careless Rapture* and *Crest of the Wave*, was another American, Dorothy Dickson, who had begun her career as a Broadway dancer. Dancing rather than singing remained her *forte*, but she had a charming voice, a lightness of touch and the striking looks that were essential to a romantic lead. Her equally beautiful daughter, Dorothy Hyson, was to marry one of Britain's leading classical actors and film stars, Sir Anthony Quayle.

In *Glamorous Night* and *Arc de Triomphe* Ivor cast a very different, but equally American talent, Elizabeth Welch. A black singer, she found, like many African-Americans, that it was easier to pursue a career in Europe than in the States, especially given the example of the phenomenally popular (and rich) Josephine Baker. Discovered by Cole Porter, she was a talent Ivor was determined to use, whatever the plot of his musical, so he wrote her in as a stowaway on a glamorous liner that sank, in a blaze of special effects, on the vast stage of the Theatre Royal, Drury Lane.

Her presence in the show was entirely extraneous, but she was at least given a showcase for her talent - a gesture on Ivor's part that was both typically generous and typically astute, for he knew that she would be an ornament to his production. Perhaps her best number was the lilting *Shanty Town*, in which Miss Welch sang of her lover far away on a Caribbean island.

If shanty towns and palm-fringed isles seem ridiculously romantic and escapist, it must not be forgotten that Ivor's shows also included very modern settings - such as the beauty salon frequented by society ladies in *Careless Rapture*, and the bustling fairground scene, set on London's Hampstead Heath in the same musical. The liner in *Glamorous Night* represented the latest in the travel chic that led to a golden age of art deco floating palaces between the two world wars.

It was on such a liner that Novello travelled to New York as a young man, and the harbour on the Hudson would have been a familiar sight to him, as would the restaurants and shops of Manhattan - particularly Sardi's - and the hotels. Where possible, he liked to stay at the homes of friends, for although he was incredibly generous, in terms of time and courtesy, with his legions of fans, and saw this as one of the duties of stardom, he preferred to restrict public adulation to the stage and the stage door. He was not fond of being pestered in the street, which is why he preferred to travel everywhere, however short the distance (including just around the corner from the Theatre Royal, Drury Lane, to his flat in the Aldwych), in his enormous Rolls Royce. Mind you, though he liked the privacy and comfort that this car afforded, he never forgot the value of publicity or the need (those were the days!) to keep up appearances, so he always had the Rolls driven by his chauffeur, Morgan, and had his monogram emblazoned on the car's doors.

This desire to preserve his distance from the fans when off duty extended to hotels. When holidaying in England (which was fairly rare, as he preferred to escape to the sun - hence his home in Jamaica) he would sometimes stay in a small, family run hotel rather than somewhere grand, but pay for all the rooms at once, ensuring that the place was packed with friends, thus keeping out unwanted attention from strangers. He made an exception in New York, however, for if he couldn't stay at a friend's flat then he stayed at the Algonquin, enjoying its style and artistic atmosphere.

One of Ivor's last holidays was in the winter of 1950/1951, when he went to Jamaica via New York, in order to get some much needed rest and sunshine. His last great hit, *King's Rhapsody*, had been playing to packed houses at the Palace Theatre (where *Les Misérables* has been running since 1984) and he wanted a break - not least because he had also been working on his final show (written for Cicely Courtneidge, and in which he didn't appear), called *Gay's The Word*.

Shortly after *Gay's the Word* opened at the Savile Theatre in upper Shaftesbury Avenue (it is now a cinema) Ivor gave his last performance in *King's Rhapsody*, on the evening of 5th March 1951. After the show he was driven in the Rolls back to the flat, where he met Tom Arnold, the producer of most of his shows. They had the inevitable bottle of champagne and discussed show business matters and theatrical gossip - both subjects dear to Ivor's heart.

That heart, which was universally acknowledged to be the most generous in the British theatre, finally beat its last after a heart attack in the early hours of 6th March. His friends, Bobby Andrews and Olive Gilbert, who appeared with him in many shows, and who were pillars of his private as well as professional life, were with him. They called a doctor, but he could do nothing.

Ivor's death marked the immediate end of his theatrical empire, and his passing marked the passing, too, of a whole musical tradition. London was almost immediately conquered by the new, post-war American musical, which Ivor had loved, learned from, but resisted - and resisted successfully: *King's Rhapsody* had taken the biggest box office advance in West End history, and more than held its own against *Oklahoma*.

The irony is that this composer, now seen as old fashioned and peculiarly English in style and appeal, had been so enthused, from his teens onwards, by the energy and excitement of the New York theatre scene, and had imported some of the best examples of American stage technique in order to create and maintain his own highly distinctive series of musicals. Therefore, although Ivor Novello was a highly distinctive, indeed unique writer, composer and performer, he in some ways symbolises the way that Broadway and West End have, over the years, and, despite being set up as rivals by commentators on both sides of the Atlantic, enjoyed a mutually beneficial and creative relationship which has served to enrich both theatrical cultures, and, despite their real and important differences, brought them together. It may be a long distance relationship, but its a relationship all the same, and one that continues to flourish, to the benefit of both the West End and of Broadway.

There is as much difference between the stage and the films as between a piano and a violin. Normally you can't become a virtuoso in both.

Ethel Barrymore 1956

You need three things in the theatre - the play, the actors and the audience, and each must give something.

Ken Haigh 1958

CHAPTER SEVEN

CAMERON MACKINTOSH AND ANDREW LLOYD WEBBER

Broadway has seen its fair share of successful impresarios down the years. The most famous still remains Florenz Ziegfeld, whose showgirls and spectacular scenery still define an age of glamour for us, some sixty years after his heyday. Yet of all the well-heeled cigar-chomping men who have left their mark on the Great White Way, the most successful, and still the most influential, after some fifteen years at the top, is a Briton. Well, with a name like Cameron Mackintosh it would be rather impertinent to describe him as an Englishman!

Yet, although he is undeniably British, and proud of it, the richest showman of the century has a life story that reads like a piece of the American Dream.

Born in 1946, into a comfortably-off family, he decided as a child that he was going to have a career in the theatre. Not as an actor, singer, or dancer, or any of the obviously attractive, public sides of show business, but as a producer. And not just a producer, but a producer of musicals.

This ambition came to him when he was eight years old (as he proudly recounts in his *Who's Who* entry). The show that sparked this desire was *Salad Days*, Julian Slade's charming musical about a magic piano and a young couple in love, that was one of the hits of the London stage in the early 1950s. The show was revived in the late 1990s, at the Vaudeville theatre, in a production that was directed by Ned Sherrin, the theatre historian, director, raconteur and wit. Cameron Mackintosh turned up at the first night in full highland gear, including a kilt!

The impresario-to-be began his theatre career as a student at the Central School of Speech and Drama, but dropped out to get some practical experience - a much more American than British thing to do.

He started as a stage hand at the Theatre Royal, Drury Lane. Although the job was a menial one, it at least meant that he was, at an early age, earning a living - however meagre - in show business. And where better to start than Drury Lane, the home of so many great British musicals, from Noel Coward's *Cavalcade*, through the extraordinary run of Ivor Novello hits in the 1930s - *Glamorous Night, Careless Rapture, Crest of the Wave*, and, of course, *The Dancing Years*. Later it had been the home of *My Fair Lady*, and little did the actresses who noticed the young stage hand with the big brown eyes realise the one day he would break box-office records as producer of a show - *Miss Saigon*.

The run of shows that was to make him one of the richest men in the world (with an estimated fortune of some three quarters of a billion dollars), and which was celebrated by an extraordinary, star-studded tribute to him at the Lyceum Theatre in London's West End (*Hey Mr Producer*, 1998) began in a relatively low key, with *Little Women* in 1967, but in 1969 he tried his first London musical, *Anything Goes*.

He experimented with many shows, suffering the usual slings and arrows that fortune throws at producers, but was convinced that he would, indeed, make his fortune. The theme of this book has been the close connection between the English and American stage, and it was, appropriately, through an American composer that Sir Cameron (he was knighted by the Queen in 1996) made his mark. This was through his production of *Side by Side* by Sondheim, in 1976.

Sondheim has long been a very popular composer and lyricist in England, a fact attested both by the number of commercial productions of his work mounted in the West End over the years, and by the fondness for his work that the National Theatre has demonstrated, with critically acclaimed performances, for example, of *Sweeny Todd* and, in 1995, with Dame Judi Dench and the marvellous Sian Philips (ex wife of Peter O'Toole), of *A Little Night Music*.

Sir Cameron returned to his British roots almost immediately, however, putting his Sondheim profits into a production of Lionel Bart's *Oliver!*, a show that he revived, in a new version, at the London Palladium in 1994. One of the several stars to play Fagin was Jonathan Pryce (of whom more later), another was Jim Dale. Dale, initially famous as a member of the *Carry On* team (the *Carry On* series being an enormous popular series of film comedies from the late 1950s to the mid-1970s, and at its heyday in the 1960s), went on to a very distinguished stage career in America, yet another on the long roll-call of British acting talent that, despite success at home, has found a niche in New York.

By 1994, Lionel Bart had long since sold his rights to the show, but Sir Cameron insisted not only on bringing him into the production at a very early stage, but gave him a cut of the profits too. This is a typical gesture of his, characterised in two ways. First, he is a generous man who has given a great deal of money to charity, particularly that associated with theatre. Secondly, having had so much fun as well as having made so much money from the business, he is a strong believer in putting something back in. This takes the form not just of employing, directly and indirectly, huge numbers of people in productions all over the world, but in conserving Britain's theatrical heritage, and reminding the young of its existence.

Two examples of this will have to suffice: first that he bought much of the memorabilia and theatre collections of the now defunct theatrical firm, H M Tennent, which had dominated the West End from the 1930s to the 1970s, giving the collection to the theatre museum; second, that he has endowed a professorship of contemporary theatre at Oxford University, so that the giants of the West End stage can share their experience with a new generation of actors, designers - and, of course, impresarios. One of the greatest living British impresarios, Michael Codron, was one of the first people to be honoured by this one-year long appointment.

Although Sir Cameron continued to produce tried and tested shows like *My Fair Lady* and *Oklahoma!*, it was a new and in many ways apparently foolhardy venture that raised him from comfortable success to fame and enormous wealth. The show was *Cats*, the year was 1981, the composer was Andrew Lloyd Webber (later Sir Andrew, now Lord Lloyd Webber, a great honour - in every sense - that recognises his remarkable contribution to the stage musical, and to the Inland Revenue!).

Lloyd Webber had, with his lyricist Tim Rice, had successes with *Joseph and his Amazing Technicolor Dream Coat*, and *Jesus Christ, Superstar*. Although they had biblical themes, the stories were well-known, the music innovative, attractive and accessible. Turning a collection of T S Eliot's poems about cats into a major West End musical was another matter altogether, and Lloyd Webber was risking his bank balance as well as his reputation on the show - as was Mackintosh.

Even here, however, there is an American connection, for T S Eliot was, of course, an American, though he came to make England his home.

So when Americans complained that *Cats* started a new trend in British musicals dominating dear old Broadway, reversing the trend of fifty years of American triumphs, it should have been noted that the lyricist and inspiration for the show had at least been born in America!

Sir Cameron's rise seemed unstoppable once he teamed up with Andrew Lloyd Webber. After producing *Song and Dance* in 1982, he went his own way, with *Blondel* (lyricist Tim Rice) and *Little Shop of Horrors*, the latter demonstrating his affection for (and shrewd judgement over) quirky small scale shows that nonetheless had great popular appeal. His affection for British composers, as well as shows that reflected a nostalgia for bygone days, was demonstrated by his backing a production of Sandy Wilson's wonderful tribute to the 1920s, *The Boyfriend*, in 1984.

The mid-1980s were to see Sir Cameron's next big success, with *Les Misérables* directed by Trevor Nunn. Still running at the Palace Theatre (owned by Lord Lloyd Webber's company, the entertainingly named Really Useful Group), *Les Misérables* was an international sensation. Its success is a tribute to Sir Cameron's judgement, but the run of the musical in New York has also demonstrated the ruthlessness that is a vital ingredient for success in the theatre - or in any business, for that matter.

After the show had been running for many years on Broadway, he decided that it was getting a little tired, and that new blood was needed. Some of the French revolutionary students had been in the production for years, and he decided to replace them with new actors. This caused a storm of protest from the cast members who had been given their marching orders, but Sir Cameron stood firm, and public opinion seemed to side with him, and there were several references made to the fact that the *Misérables* students were beginning to look rather mature for their roles. Whatever the rights or wrongs of individual cases, he was surely right in principle, in that there is no such thing as a guaranteed long-term job in the theatre - or in any business, for that matter. Even the longest running show in the world, Agatha Christie's *The Mousetrap* (originally at the Ambassador's Theatre, now at the neighbouring St Martin's) has a complete cast change once a year to keep the play (first produced in 1952) fresh!

This ruthlessness was displayed a few years later when *Miss Saigon*, the re-working and updating of Puccini's *Madam Butterfly* (what with *Miss Saigon* and *Rent* both being huge hits, one wonders which of Puccini's other scores will be seen as the next big modern musical?) which had been a great success in London, at the Theatre Royal, Drury Lane, where Sir Cameron had been a stagehand over twenty years before. Jonathan Pryce had earned rave reviews as the Eurasian villain of the piece, and when the show transferred to Broadway, Sir Cameron wanted him in the role in the New York production. This caused a storm on the grounds that it wasn't politically correct to have a white man playing a man of mixed race, but Cameron stuck to his guns and gave a simple ultimatum to the Broadway unions - no Pryce, no show, so no jobs and no money. The unions gave in, and Jonathan Pryce went on to have another well-deserved success. Meanwhile, *Miss Saigon* continues to attract coach-loads of customers every evening, re-fighting the Vietnam War long after the real event is long over, and the Americans, having lost the war, have easily and convincingly won the peace. The B52 bombers may have failed, but the Big Mac has undeniably triumphed.

Michael Crawford, who starred in *Phantom of the Opera* in New York, tells of his first night on Broadway as something he will never forget. He had his two young daughters with him, and as they hugged each other in his dressing room afterwards, he said, "Remember this night, it will never happen again." He said that he was featured on the nightly news as scalpers were being arrested outside the theatre. "I was not arrested, but I was in the news. 'The whole of New York will know you tomorrow,' said a New Yorker."

Sarah Brightman also starred in this production. Formerly married to Andrew Lloyd Webber, she was the toast of all New York. The following chapter describes the theatre clubs where the most prestigious thespians in New York invite the British.

CHAPTER EIGHT

FAMOUS THEATRE CLUBS: THE PLAYERS, THE LAMBS, THE FRIARS

Obviously British performers on Broadway, although working eight performances a week, are like any visitors to New York - they search out the places of interest in their free time, explore and see all that New York has to offer. There is sight-seeing, shopping, finding good restaurants and socialising with fellow-actors. Their American counterparts often entertain them at New York's famous theatre clubs.

Theatre clubs are sometimes their home away from home. Just as London has the Garrick Club, the Groucho Club and the Chelsea Arts Club, where actors, directors and writers gather, New York has the Players, the Lambs and the Friars. Any visitor to London would be fortunate to be issued an invitation to the Garrick Club; the same applies to The Players in New York. In fact, the current president of the club is British. It is part of a New York tradition to attend a "Roast" at the Friars Club, and many an actor has been honoured with a dinner at the Players, and then been able to watch a performance on the small stage at the end of the dining room.

Sir John Gielgud said that The Players was his second home when he was working on Broadway.

The Players Club

The Players Club in Gramercy Park has a unique library of books about thespians and records of most of New York's theatre history, including famous first nights with the great names of British legends on Broadway, from Henry Irving, Ellen Terry and Laurence Olivier to the present day. Lynn Redgrave became the first woman President of the club in the early 1990s for a brief time while she was in New York. The current President is the British actor, Michael Allinson, and the Executive Director is John Martello.

The Players is in downtown New York on the south side of Gramercy Park, in the centre of which stands a full-length bronze statue of Edwin Booth as Hamlet on top of a granite pedestal. Here is an extract from Dan Poole's history of The Players.

Step down to the entrance of No 16 Gramercy Park, beneath a covered stone loggia from which project immense wrought-iron, Renaissance-style working gas lanterns, and enter the well-preserved nineteenth-century world of Edwin Booth.

The greatest American actor of his time, Booth bought the 1845 Gothic Revival-style house in early 1888 and commissioned architect, Stanford White, to transform it into a clubhouse suitable, in Booth's words, for "social intercourse between the representative members of the Dramatic profession, and of the kindred professions of Literature, Painting, Sculpture, and Music, and the Patrons of the Arts ..."

The Players opened as a club at midnight on New Year's Eve in 1888, and for more than a century it has fulfilled not only that goal but another objective set forth by Booth at the same time: " ... and the creation of a library relating especially to the history of the American Stage and the preservation of pictures, bills of the play, photographs, and curiosities, connected with such history."

From the foyer of the clubhouse, the dark-wood stairway is open to the fifth-floor skylight, and its ornately carved mahogany newel posts begin with a spotlighted bust of Shakespeare.

The Grill Room

Down a few steps and through the glass doors is the Grill Room, where several generations of actors, artists, writers and others have gathered for conversation and refreshment. A focal point is the table where Samuel L Clemens (Mark Twain) often shot pool with other founders of the club. His pool cue is displayed over his portrait above the fireplace, as are those of Frank Morgan, Franklin Pierce Adams and others.

Art works on every wall of the Grill Room include Marshall Goodman's water-colours of the club's past presidents and another by him of Michael Allinson. Here, too, are Norman Rockwell's portrait of Charles Coburn, John Barrymore's water-colours of the sets of *Hamlet*, James Cagney's drawing of Roland Winters, Thomas Nast's *Tammany Tiger* and Al Hirschfeld's drawing of Edwin Booth (the only one he has ever done of an actor who wasn't alive when he drew it).

Near the Grill room is the Sarah Bernhardt Room; it is a tiny ancient elevator, still in use, and so-called because the great actress became trapped in it for an hour or so one evening in 1911 while visiting the club as a guest.

The First Floor

Art treasures line the wall space along the entire expanse of the building's open stairway. Leading up the entrance staircase to the Great Hall are portraits of John Henry Wallack, Edwin Forrest and many others.

The Great Hall, on the first floor of The Players, is dominated by a massive fireplace designed by Stanford White to incorporate the club's seal with its masks of comedy and tragedy. Over the fireplace mantel hangs a painting by Robert Sully of Edwin Booth's father, Junius Brutus Booth, made up as Hamlet.

It is in the Great Hall where players and their guests gather for receptions preceding Thursday dinners, Tuesday special entertainment evenings, and traditional black-tie events such as Founders' Night, New Year's Eve and the Pipe Nights, when great actors and others eminent in their fields are saluted for their work.

Paintings of the club's first president, Edwin Booth, posing as Richelieu, and of its second president, actor Joseph Jefferson in *The Rivals*, face each other at the entrance to the Dining Room, and a picture of Booth as Hamlet dominates the wall opposite the fireplace at the head of the stairs.

The Sargent Room, at the north end of the Great Hall, features oil paintings of three of the club's founders by John Singer Sargent, the best-known American portrait artist of the Victorian age. A full-length study of Edwin Booth, hanging over the fireplace, is flanked by portraits of Lawrence Barrett on the left and Joseph Jefferson on the right.

Just inside the room is the oak Savonarola throne-chair in which John Barrymore sat when he did his great Hamlet in 1922, and above it is his portrait.

The Dining Room, to the south of the Great Hall, is where the club's major events take place. At the far end of the room is an informal stage used frequently for performances and play readings.

The Second Floor

Along the stairway to the second floor are portraits of actresses such as Katherine Hepburn, Muriel Kirkland and Beatrice Lillie, as well as James Montgomery Flagg's pencil sketch of Rosalind Russell. A tall eighteenth century English oak case clock stands on the landing, beside an interior window depicting the masks of comedy and tragedy.

Near the entrance to the Library stands a door bearing a plaque which reads: "In this room during the first three months of 1913 there met without permission the small committee of four or five which ultimately led to the formation of the Actors' Equity Association."

The Library, officially named the Hampden-Booth Theatre Library after its principal donors, now occupies what originally were two large rooms at the front of the second floor, each with its own fireplace and mantel of red African marble. Over one mantel is a quotation from *The Tempest*: "My library was dukedom large enough for me." Over the other is a quotation from *Titus Andronicus*: "Take choice of all my library."

There is a growing collection of books, manuscripts, photographs, prompt scripts, notebooks and more than 50,000 plays and many old quartos of early dramatists.

In 1957, the Library was chartered by the State of New York as an educational institution and two years later it officially opened its doors for the first time to qualified researchers and students of the theatre. Today the Hampden-Booth Theatre Library is considered the finest repository of theatre references, art and memorabilia of its kind.

The Card Room, at the far end of the second floor hallway, is used for private functions and committee meetings. It displays the poker table said to have been used by Mark Twain, portraits of James Cagney and Douglas Fairbanks Sr, and a photograph of three Cyranos, Walter Hampden, Jose Ferrer and Jimmy Durante.

The Third Floor

At the top of the stairs to the third floor are cases containing costumes Edwin Booth wore as Iago, Othello, Richard III, Hamlet, Macbeth and in other roles. And the life mask of Ellen Terry faces a photograph nearby of her great-nephew John Gielgud in his 1936 role as Hamlet.

The Booth Room, at the front of the third floor, was called by Booth his "nest among the treetops of Gramercy Park". This is the suite, a parlour and a bedroom, where he lived his final five years after the opening of The Players. The rooms have been left furnished as they were when he died in 1893 at age fifty-nine, including several of the pipes and cigars he loved so much. The gasolier hanging over the dining table in the parlour still works, and occasionally it is lit.

Here still are many of Booth's personal treasures, reminders of his great theatrical career and of his family tragedies. In the far corner of the parlour near a window is a painting of his first wife and great love, the beautiful actress, Mary Devlin, who died so young after only three years of marriage. Beneath her portrait is a bookcase, atop which rest memorabilia such as the skull of Yorick which Booth saluted hundreds of times while playing

64

Hamlet. The skull is said to be that of a horse thief who asked just before being hanged that his skull be forwarded to Booth's father, whom he admired.

Between the parlour windows, a bust of Shakespeare looks down over Booth's roll-top desk and over it is a copy of the legend on Shakespeare's tomb at Stratford. On the table are Booth's cigar case, a bronze casting of his daughter Edwina's hand in his, and the book of poetry by William Winter open to the page he was reading before he died.

In the bedroom are the actor's brass bed with its faded silk coverlet and its canopy of yellow satin, and beside it rest his slippers. Near the window is his Queen Anne-style ebony wood chaise, and at its foot sits the oak make-up case he took on his tours. Beneath the window is his dressing table, and against another wall is a Chippendale bureau. On the wall behind the chaise is a shadow-box tribute to Booth.

In this personal retreat, where the great actor lived out his last years and died, can be found his continuing spirit, the essence of his life. But Edwin Booth lives to this day in every room and on every floor of The Players, the club he founded and loved.

John Gielgud said, "I have the happiest memories of the Players Club where dinners were given for me and for the Lunts also." Laurence Olivier remembered it fondly too.

The Lambs Club

The Lambs traces its lineage to early nineteenth century London. "In those far off days the home of Charles Lamb, essayist, critic and leader in London's literary life, was a rendezvous for luminaries in the world of arts and letters.Numbered among them were the men of that period's vigorous and thriving theatre..." writes Lewis J Hardee, the Club historian, who gave me this report. Charles and his sister, Mary Lamb, maintained a lively salon where could be found good conversation, good drink, and good fellowship. In 1869 a small group of actors and men about town decided to form a private dinner club, a popular idea of the day. John Hare, a veteran actor, is credited with having conceived the club. Tradition has it that when debating the choice of a name for the new fraternity, someone recalled their happy visits to The Lambs' salon when invariably someone would exclaim, "Let's go round to The Lambs!" Thus, "The Lambs".

The London Lambs held its first weekly dinner on 16th October, 1869, at the Gaiety Restaurant. It thrived for ten years when "The Lambs grew into old sheep and strayed from the Fold. Some died. Some married." In the meantime, in 1874, one of their number, actor Henry J Montague, came to New York on a professional engagement. Henry Montague cut a dapper figure about town. With good looks, a knack for light comedy, and plenty of opportunity in the emerging New York theatre, he had a bright and promising future before him. He would found the New York Lambs.

At Christmas time in 1874, George McLean hosted a supper party for his theatre friends at the Blue Room of fashionable Delmonico's Restaurant. His guests were Arthur Wallack, Henry J Montague, Harry Beckett and Edward Arnott. The evening proved so agreeable that it was decided to meet on a regular monthly basis. After the festivities had gone on for nearly two and a half years, Henry Montague suggested that the little club be called The Lambs, after the club in London to which he had belonged.

As the nation goes, so goes Broadway; as Broadway goes, so goes The Lambs. The history of this great club has been directly connected to Broadway, the New York theatre from which it sprang, and, like Broadway, its fortunes have had many ups and downs. As Broadway grew from a fledgling, clumsy business to a dynamic industry, so did The Lambs; as Broadway has had its triumphs and tragedies, so has The Lambs. Their destinies were linked at birth.

By 1874 the theatre district had migrated from the Wall Street area to Broadway between Union and Herald Squares. Theatre fare was abundant and varied. J. Lester Wallack's Theatre, at 13th and Broadway, boasted classy French and English farces; Tony Pastor's on 14th Street provided the best in variety entertainment; the last of the great minstrels were at Bryant's; and opera reigned on 14th Street at The Academy of Music. Harrigan and Hart offered Irish and German tenement humour at their various theatres. Booth's Theatre, at the south-east corner of 6th Avenue and 23rd Street, provided stars domestic and foreign, and of course, Shakespeare.

The Lambs is the oldest theatrical society in America. For over one hundred and twenty-three years it has been central to New York theatre. Its fame is global. ASCAP and Actors' Equity were conceived there. Since its founding in 1874, its membership has included actors, producers, playwrights, composers, directors and lovers of theatre in general. Its roster of members reads like a Who's Who in the entertainment world - George M Cohan, Al Jolson, John Philip Sousa, Victor Herbert, Will Rogers, David Belasco, W C Fields, Walter Cronkite, Eugene O'Neill, Irving Berlin, Oscar Hammerstein II, Sigmund Romberg, Alan J Lerner and Frederick Loewe,

Cecil B De Mille, Douglas Fairbanks, Eddie Foy, both Sr and Jr, Bert Lahr, Bert Wheeler, Fred Astaire, and Spencer Tracy, to name a few. Honorary members have included Col Charles Lindbergh, Hon Thomas E Dewey, Dwight D Eisenhower and John Wayne. Richard L Charles, actor and publisher, is the incumbent Shepherd of The Lambs. His wife, Joyce Randolph (Trixie of TV's *The Honeymooners* fame) is a regular. Shepherd Emeritus Tom Dillon is President of the Actors' Fund of America.

The New York of 1874 was a city bursting with energy, optimism, and a rapidly exploding population. In 1870 its population stood at a million; by the end of the century it would triple in size. It extended from the Battery to 59th Street, beyond which were farms and land only just then being eyed by developers. It was a city whose skyline was spiked with church steeples and the masts of tall ships. Horse-drawn omnibuses and carriages rattled noisily and dustily through the busy streets. It was the Gaslight Era, when women wore bustles, when great hordes of immigrants disembarked from fleets of ships from Europe, when whiskey went for five cents a glass. Many of the great landmarks of New York were making their appearances on the scene - the American Museum of Natural History, the Metropolitan Museum of Art, the Brooklyn Bridge, the Statue of Liberty. Elevated railroad lines were rising above the streets, spewing from overhead their hot cinders over First, Second, Third Sixth and Ninth Avenues.

Maurice, the father of John Barrymore, almost made The Lambs Club his home (as did John Drew The Players). There he could fend off bores.

"Don't you recognise me, Mr Barrymore?"

"I didn't at first, but when you didn't buy I knew you right away."

Told by a friend he must see E H Southern's *Hamlet*, he replied, "My boy, I don't encourage vice."

At the close of the old century men of great prestige had been added to The Lambs' membership, including the celebrated actor, Sir Henry Irving, General Horace Porter of Civil War fame, Charles A Dana, and Dion Bouccicault. The fortunes of the club began to soar.

The old traditions continue. Throughout the year The Lambs presents variety shows, plays, musicals and other entertainments. The weekly Happy Hour features impromptu Low Jinks, and conclude with the traditional joining of hands to sing "Baa, Baa, Baa". Annual outings are held at the Actors' Fund Home in Englewood, New Jersey. In its private rooms members enjoy pool, socialising, or rehearsing for auditions. The Foundation continues its important work.

The Friars Club

Many British performers working on Broadway are invited to the Friars. In the past they have rubbed shoulders with Frank Sinatra, Yul Brynner, Elizabeth Taylor and Mike Todd. The history of the actual Clubhouse (provided by the Club) is included, as it is an interesting story of one of New York's famous theatrical establishments.

Whether it be a wisecrack or a wicked witticism, a song or a dance, the ultimate in the arts is found within the doors of 57 East 55th Street.

Gathered each day in this five-story brownstone building are the best and brightest of show business, the world's top headliners telling tales among themselves while enjoying the Club's excellent facilities, exquisite surroundings and superb cuisine.

This English Renaissance structure known as "The Monastery" is home to the New York Friars Club, a fraternal organisation with an honoured reputation for excellence in performance and public service. Reciting the long roster of luminaries who have graced the Friars would give a name-dropper laryngitis. In a tradition that started at the turn of the century under the leadership of George M Cohan, The Friars Club has attracted the elite of show business as well as distinguished industry leaders through the years. The exalted position of Abbot has been held by such legends as George M Cohan, George Jessel, Mike Todd, Milton Berle, Joe E. Lewis, Ed Sullivan and Frank Sinatra.

The greatest songwriter of all time, Irving Berlin, wrote Alexander's Ragtime Band for the first Friars Frolic in 1911. Other early Members include heavyweight champions Jack "Manassa Mauler" Dempsey and Gentleman Jim Corbett.

They are fierce in their dedication to the sick and the needy, and throughout their long and honourable history the Friars have, through their Celebrity Luncheons, Roasts and Testimonial Dinners, raised millions of dollars for worthy causes. Abbot Frank Sinatra said, "Their continuous good work for charity rather than their great triumphs on the stages of the world is the true glory of this band of earthly angels known as the New York Friars."

For years, women were not permitted to enter the interior of the Friars Monastery. At the Clubhouse on 48th Street, there was a small cubicle at the entrance of the building and it was not unusual to see women performers like Gracie Allen (Burns and Allen), Mary Livingston Benny and Eva Sully (Block and Sully), sitting in the little reception area waiting for their husbands, George Burns, Jack Benny and Jesse Block, three close friends, to join them as they left the Club. Subsequently, on 56th Street and in the present Monastery, the rules have been changed to permit women in the Clubhouse after four p.m.

A new era was welcomed at the New York Friars in 1988 with the admission of women as full-fledged members. Liza Minnelli was the first woman to apply for membership and the first admitted. She was followed by such shining stars as Carol Burnett, Phyllis Diller, Edie Gorme, Anjelica Huston, Martha Raye, Joan Rivers, Brooke Shields, Dinah Shore, Barbara Sinatra, Barbara Streisand and Elizabeth Taylor. Soon after gaining admittance, Rivers joked that, "the Club is so nice, I'm thinking of making it an all-women's organisation." There have been many changes since the Club's inception in 1904, but throughout the century it has remained devoted to the original purpose of providing a warm and comfortable environment for the entertainment industry. Of the Club's 1,400 members, two-thirds must be involved in show business related activities. The remaining one-third of the membership consists of prominent individuals from the corporate world.

The Club traces its beginnings back to a group of theatrical publicists who called a meeting of the Press Agents' Association at Browne's Chop House. They were concerned about the huge amount of complimentary tickets being distributed by theatres, as well as other abuses that threatened the stability of their industry, meeting each Friday, the group eventually reached agreements with producers, managers and box office treasurers to correct the situation. Two years later, at another meeting in Keene's Chop House, the scope of the organisation was expanded to include press agents from around the country along with a wider spectrum of the theatrical industry.

At this time the name Friars was adopted to express the more fraternal purpose of the organisation. Frederick F Schrader is credited with suggesting the name. The weekly Friday meetings were held at the Hotel Hermitage until the Friars took possession of their first building at 107 West 45th Street. The Clubhouse, which came to be known the Hermitage, was formally opened 9th May 1908. Charles Emerson Cook was named the Club's second Abbot, succeeding Wells Hawks.

The celebrated tradition of honouring personalities had already begun. In 1907 Victor Herbert, who was the Guest of Honour at a dinner, sang his speech - *Here's To The Friars* - and it has been the Friars' Anthem ever since. Herbert wrote the music and Charles Emerson Cook penned the words.

The "Friars Frolics" were the Galas of the Friars before the annual Testimonial Dinners and Celebrity Roasts became the attraction they are now. Abbot George M Cohan assembled a star-studded cast for the Frolics of 1916. The cast featured Cohan, then the King of Broadway, Will Rogers, Willie Collier, De Wolf Hopper, Irving Berlin, the first of the internationally known female impersonators, Julian Eltinge, the legendary minstrel showman, Lew Dockstader, and Victor Herbert and his Orchestra. The Frolics played sixteen cities in fourteen days. It premièred on a Sunday night at New York's New Amsterdam Theatre, and on Monday a matinee was played in Philadelphia and a special command performance took place later that same night in Washington, DC for President Woodrow Wilson on the stage of the old Ford Theatre where Lincoln was shot.

When the curtain came down, President Wilson went backstage to personally thank the cast. Right there and then, Abbot Cohan introduced a resolution which was carried unanimously, electing President Woodrow Wilson as the first Honorary Member, and he accepted the gesture most graciously.

George M Cohan, one of America's great songwriters and entertainers, was installed as Abbot in 1912. With the exception of two years, 1920 and 1927, it was a post he held through to 1932.

With the proceeds of the Frolics' road tour, Cohan spurred the drive to build a new Clubhouse on West 48th Street, and he hired architect Harry Alan Jacobs to design the new building for the Friars Club. The style of the exterior was Tudor Gothic. The large windows on the second floor frankly expressed the dignified banquet hall, as it was the chief feature of the building. Here, the Friars held their entertainment. Naturally, because the Club Members belonged mostly to the theatrical profession, this room was the centre of the entire plan, where the Friars continued to perform their sketches, impromptu entertainment and their famous Testimonial Dinners for Members and friends.

The new Monastery at 106 West 48th Street was officially opened on 22nd May 1916, with fitting pomp and ceremony. Our Abbot, George M Cohan, led the procession from the old Monastery to the new quarters, where he broke a bottle of sparkling American wine on the cornerstone and declared, "I dedicate our Friars Club to Art, Literature and Good Fellowship." More than 500 Friars attended the opening banquet and the program that evening included performances by legendary stars of the day.

The building was considered to be the most handsome Clubhouse in New York City, modern in every detail while still retaining the intimate characteristics so essential to a fraternal group.

The Club continued to prosper. On 1st May 1916, there were 658 active members, 292 lay members, 258 non-residents and four members in the military service. The total membership represented an increase of 282 in one year.

The annual Frolics, staged in the Grand Hall of the Monastery, played before SRO audiences. Among those honoured at various dinners were Mayor Jimmy Walker, Governor Alfred E Smith, Lee Shubert, Oscar Hammerstein, George M Cohan, David Belasco, Irving Berlin, John Ringling, Mary Pickford and Douglas Fairbanks, and Enrico Caruso. The first woman roasted by the Friars was Sophie Tucker in 1953. No other club has been as successful in attracting such a distinguished company of intellectual and notable personalities at its functions.

The Friars boasts of two Members, George M Cohan and Irving Berlin, who were honoured by Presidents of the United States with the "Congressional Medal of Honor". Cohan wrote the famed World War I song, *Over There,* in the original Friars Clubhouse.

Hard times struck the Friars, and the whole of the world in 1932. The depression, the demise of vaudeville and a mass trek westward to Hollywood by many stars seeking work in the film industry, decimated the ranks of Friars. The trade paper, *Variety,* reported an incident that took place during those years of financial strain. A produce purveyor who was owed some $600 by the Friars went to court and obtained a judgement to have a padlock placed on the Monastery until he got paid. Harry Hershfield, a great humorist of this time, was the Treasurer and he appealed to the court to have the padlock removed. When the Judge suggested to Hershfield that members' dues be raised, Hershfield replied, "The Members don't want to owe any more money." Somehow, the money was raised and the padlock was removed.

Eventually, the 48th Street Clubhouse was abandoned, although a hard core of the membership continued to operate the organisation at various sites, first in the Lindy's building at 51st Street and Broadway and later at the Hotel Edison. It wasn't until 1948 that a new home was found when then Abbot Milton Berle and Treasurer-Legal Secretary Louis P Randell negotiated for the Clubhouse at 128 West 56th Street.

In 1956, Abbot Emeritus Milton Berle, Abbot Joe E Lewis, Dean Harry Delf, and the members decided to purchase another new Clubhouse. The building they selected is our present headquarters at 57 East 55th Street, and this beautifully designed structure has remained the home of the Friars ever since.

The move to the new Clubhouse marked the beginning of the Club's most successful era. Major alterations have been made from the basement to the roof to make the Clubhouse what it is today. The first floor contains the main dining room and the Round-the-World bar, renamed the William

B Williams lounge in memory of the former Dean. The second floor houses the Milton Berle Room and the Joe E Lewis Bar, while the third floor consists of the Ed Sullivan Room, the Frank Sinatra Room and the George Burns Cardroom. The Billiard Room, named after former Dean, Harry Delf, and the Barber Shop are on the fourth floor. The fifth floor contains the well-equipped Health Club, named after former Dean, Buddy Howe.

It has been the tradition of the Friars Club to honour its deceased Members with plaques on the back of the chairs in the main dining room. Periodically the names are changed but the illustrious names live forever. Among past Friars whose names have been immortalised are: Edward F Albee, Yul Brynner, Eddie Cantor, Bing Crosby, Jimmy Durante, Douglas Fairbanks, W C Fields, Oscar Hammerstein, George Jessel, Harry Hershfield, Al Jolson, Ted Lewis, Edward R Murrow, Will Rogers, Lee Shubert, Joe Smith, Ed Sullivan, Mike Todd, Richard Tucker, James J Walker and Walter Winchell.

The Friars Club is considered to be one of the top-rated clubs in the country. The Club is famous world-wide for its Celebrity Roasts and Testimonial Dinners honouring the stars of show business, The famed Celebrity Roast, which features the greats of the entertainment world taking their best barbs at a Guest of Honour, is the most imitated function throughout the country. Moreover, the format has been used on a number of television shows.

History of the Clubhouse

The present home of the Friars Club at 57 East 55th Street, New York City, was known from the time of its construction in 1909 to its sale in 1937 as the Martin Erdmann Residence. A five-story English Renaissance house, it is considered by contemporary critics to be a capable and clever work of architecture. The decade in which it was erected was one of tremendous building activity on the part of wealthy merchants, manufacturers and bankers. Andrew Carnegie, William Payne Whitney, the Astors, F W Woolworth, and many others undertook the task of building palatial residences. Occasionally, the result was a noble monument to the derivative genius of some American architect trained in Europe and given freedom to create. Such was undoubtedly the case with the Erdmann Residence.

The late Mr Martin Erdmann was a bachelor, and a collector of English mezzotints, who engaged the architectural firm of Taylor and Levi in 1908 to build a home for himself and his valuable art collection. He purchased two plots of ground on East 55th Street, each having a frontage of sixteen-and-one-half feet. The plots were occupied by a four-story brownstone house which was torn down to make room for the new structure. The location was considered to be a fine residential section, which had been guaranteed a dignified development by the inclusion of restrictive clauses in all of the property deeds, forbidding the establishment of such nuisances as livery stables, breweries, tanneries, forge or blacksmith shops, glue factories, ink or vitriol manufactures, and other similar trades of equally noisome character. These restrictions still remain in the property deed acquired by the Friars Club.

The floor plan of the house was conditioned by the needs of a bachelor client as opposed to the needs of a family, and hence it differs somewhat from the conventional residence. After the floor-plan was approved, the architects made sketches for the exterior facade in several styles including Georgian, Colonial, Elizabethan and English Renaissance. The client chose the English Renaissance plan and the work of designing the interior in that style began. Mr Erdmann commissioned the architects to design every detail of the house including not only the panelling, the designs for the carving of the balustrades, mouldings, cornices, doors and door-frames, the chandeliers, and iron work, but also the interior furnishings and draperies. As Mr Levi, one of the architects, explained, "We designed everything but the mezzotints and the oriental rugs." Three years passed from the time of the drawing of the first sketch to the completion of the furnishings. Everything in the house is real and genuine, as neither Mr Erdmann nor the architects would tolerate the use of shams or imitations.

The house is spacious, well-built, and well preserved. It contains a wealth of beautiful architectural details, worthy of study, from the vaulted ceiling of its dignified marble entrance hall, to the minutest detail of wood carving in the wall panels and in the magnificent railing leading from the second to the third floors. The English Renaissance decor is never fussy, overdone, or flamboyant. With a preponderance of oak panelling of simple design, and with restraint in the use of decorative pattern, the house is truly masculine in character. Both stylistically and architecturally, it gives promise of enduring time with a minimum of attention.

Two far-sighted provisions made by the original owner benefit the Friars Club. First, great care was taken to make the building completely fireproof. According to the architects, it was considered the most fireproof residence in Manhattan and incidentally resulted in the lowest possible fire insurance rate for Mr Erdmann. In addition, provision was made for a complete furnace system and all the necessary arrangements made for the utilisation of steam heat supplied by the New York Steam Company. The latter provision, which was an unusual one at the time of the construction, eliminated the handling of dangerous fuels and ashes on the premises.

After Mr Erdmann's death, his estate sold the house in 1937 to Mr Frederick Brown, a prominent New York real estate broker, who bought it as an investment and who held it until the American Institute of Physics purchased it in August 1943.

The home of the Friars is situated in what is known to today's real estate brokers as a protected area. All around the Clubhouse are developments which preclude the possibility of the neighbourhood becoming a blighted area. Within close vicinity of Rockefeller Centre, Fifth, Park and Madison Avenues, and Central Park, they all guarantee that land values will remain high. For the most part, these developments have risen within the past one hundred years. Fifth Avenue, which a century ago was called Middle Road above Forty-Second Street, changed from country land to fashionable residential street and then to a fashionable business avenue. Central Park has lent prestige to the north-central section of Manhattan since its construction in 1857. The Friars Club, located close to the centre of this favoured area, benefits by the proximity of these great investments, With its distinguished past and promising future, it will remain an interesting and prominent edifice for many decades.

A novelist may lose his readers for a few pages; a playwright
never dares lose his audience for a minute.

Terence Rattigan, *New York Journal-American*, 1956

Chapter Nine

Celebrated Theatrical Restaurants and Hotels

At the turn of the last century there were Churchill's, Maxim's, Delmonico's, Luchow's, the Everglades, Pabst's, Shanley's Moulin Rouge and before that Rector's. Broadway's night-life would shortly be replaced by speakeasies and gangster murders.

Rector's was the place to be seen. With huge mirrors on the walls, gilt and velvet everywhere, the decor was Louis XV; there were one hundred tables downstairs and seventy-five upstairs. Actors Edwin Booth, Fanny Kemble and Dion Boucicault were playing in the theatres. One of the most popular producers then was Charles Frohman, who preferred British plays and brought them over from England.

Rector's was between 43rd and 44th St in Times Square. Frohman said, "I found Broadway a quiet little lane of ham and eggs in 1889, and left it a full-blown avenue of lobsters and champagne." No play was a hit unless it was followed by a reception at Rector's. Sarah Bernhardt, Ellen Terry, Henry Irving, Lillie Langtry and Herbert Beerbohm Tree were seen there, Tree, even when he had received a bad review from John Palmer of his Shylock; "Go and see Shylock as Mr Tree."

The British stars rubbed shoulders at Rector's with Victor Herbert, Henry Miller and Theodore Dreiser. There is a story that George M Cohan tried to save Rector's from closing but failed.

Besides the experience of seeing the show, there is the Broadway routine. It is almost *de rigueur* to start with an early dinner or at least drinks at a famous restaurant in theatreland. Some restaurants have little flags on the tables for people going on to a show, to indicate this to the waiter. Sardi's restaurant is packed to the caricatures on the walls at seven p.m., but by curtain time at eight p.m. it is deserted. All around the streets from 42nd to 50th St is the jostling, excitement and anticipation of theatre-goers in their hundreds. No other section of a city is so focused on theatre as Broadway between 7.30 p.m. and eight on any night.

Sardi's

Sardi's on West 44th Street is legendary in the theatre world. A family business handed down from father to son, Sardi senior opened the restaurant in its current location in 1927. The caricatures on the walls show the best-known actors, actresses, playwrights and directors. Walter Winchell was one of Broadway's most powerful columnists from 1928 to 1960. He loved Sardi's, and he used to write about it in his column which was nationally syndicated, so millions of people linked Sardi's with the celebrated stars.

In Sardi's book, *Off the Wall at Sardi's*, he tells many stories about the actors who have dined there, and relates why the caricatures are precious mementoes to him. Often the stars refuse to sign their pictures, but Sardi hangs them up anyway. Because the collection is always being added to, many of the older ones are "retired". They are now in the Library of the Performing Arts at the Lincoln Centre.

When asked who was the most impressive person he had ever met in Sardi's, he said that some of them weren't in the theatre at all, President Harry Truman, Eleanor Roosevelt and, an all-time favourite, Ernie Kovacs.

Vincent says, "I don't mind not being a doctor, I'm taking care of people, but in a different way."

Vincent Sardi Jr offered credit to actors years ago, feeding them when they were fresh out of money. Jose Ferrer said that Vincent was partly responsible for his winning his Oscar for Cyrano. "By feeding me while I was financing *Cyrano* on the stage, he made it possible for me to get a movie offer and eventually to play the part on film. I ran up a bill for $1700, but Vincent never mentioned the bill."

Sardi's is the place where the "first night" parties are held. Tradition has it that the reason is because the *New York Times* is just next door, and the papers get delivered here as soon as they are printed. Careers are made and broken by the next review. The cast stay up waiting for the papers and wait for the first light of dawn. As Sardi himself said, "You can always tell how the box office is going to behave the next day by what happens in Sardi's after the reviews come out. If they're good, we start to hear, "Captain, a bottle of champagne and the food menu." If the reviews aren't good, all we hear is, "Check, please."

In his youth, Vincent played three walk-on roles on Broadway, and appeared in two television plays, in both of which he played himself with Sardi's as the setting. He still appears in the restaurant from time to time, but since a recent heart operation he spends much of his time at home in Vermont.

Sardi's is where Laurence Olivier, after his show on Broadway, dined with Noel Coward to tell him his marriage to Vivien Leigh was over. They were the "Royal Pair" at that stage. Both in London and New York they were household names.

Sardi also goes on to say that PR and press agents always want their stars to sit in the front of the restaurant, but he maintains that if they cross the room to a back table, everyone in the restaurant will see them.

The Cafe des Artistes

Situated on West 67th Street, the Cafe des Artistes is on the ground floor of an apartment building, called the Hotel des Artistes, which was home at various times to Noel Coward, Isadora Duncan and Rudolf Valentino. It is probably best known for the murals, painted in the 1930s by Howard Chandler Christy, who was initially a celebrated magazine illustrator, then a fashionable portrait painter. The murals depict pretty, nude wood-nymphs, dancing around and generally disporting themselves. The names of the paintings are: *The Parrot Girl, The Swing Girl, Ponce de Leon, Fall, Spring* and *The Fountain Girl*. In 1917, Christy was one of the earliest residents in the newly-built Hotel des Artistes - which is not a hotel, but a residential building along the lines of Parisian mansions. It originally housed a private ballroom, a swimming pool and a squash court, and, of course, the famous restaurant on the ground floor.

Christy's latter profession as a society and government officials portrait painter put him in the limelight wherever he went: newspapers published interviews detailing his latest portraits, the clothes he and Mrs Christy wore and who they were with. This time, his lifestyle, not that of the people he depicted in his earlier illustrations, was what the public looked up to.

The Cafe was a meeting place between creative efforts, offering reasonably priced food flavoured with good conversation; and it also served an essential function for residents of the Hotel des Artistes. Because the sumptuous duplexes had only tiny Pullman kitchens, the famed tenants bought their own raw ingredients, sent them down to the kitchen of the Cafe des Artistes with instructions for cooking, and the kitchen then sent dinners upstairs on dumbwaiters precisely at the time requested. To keep cold foods in the pantries of the apartments, a Rube Goldberg-like twenty-ton ice machine in the basement circulated frigid ice-water into each apartment's icebox.

In an era long past, Fannie Hurst, Marcel Duchamp, Maurice Maetelinck, Isadora Duncan, Alexander Woolcott, and Mayor Fiorello La Guardia had their regular tables at the Cafe.

The Cafe is now a meeting-place for some of the most famous names in the artistic and entertainment worlds. Isaac Stern, Kathleen Turner, James Levine, Itzhak Perlman and Paul Newman are among the regulars. The ambience is exceptional, perhaps the most romantic in New York, taking its tone from the care-free young nymphs frolicking in the murals and the flowers, plants and chandeliers in the main dining-room.

Elaine's

Elaine's, 1703 Second Avenue (between East 88th and 89th Streets) is the haunt of theatrical, literary and film stars. Mary Quant and Jean Muir also made it popular with British dress designers years ago. Woody Allen is a regular. Michael Caine, Clint Eastwood visit as do writers such as George Plimpton, who made it famous in one of his short stories. Elaine presides over the front tables, and you should be careful not to be seated in Siberia (the back tables). Elaine herself is a much loved restaurateur who is a patron of the arts.

Another famous spot, The Russian Tea Room on West 57th Street near Carnegie Hall is at present closed, but hopefully soon to reopen.

The Rainbow Room

On the 65th floor of the Rockefeller Centre, there is a spectacular view from one of the most romantic rooms in New York. The divided staircase descending from behind the orchestra is reminiscent of the Cafe Royal in London. One can well imagine the dramatic entrance of Marlene Dietrich or Noel Coward, descending slowly down on to the band-stand. There is a revolving dance floor, with dancing, usually to a large orchestra. Art Deco design is a continuing theme in the night-club, Rainbow in the Stars, just along the corridor. It's a night of Gershwin, Cole Porter and Jerome Kern, up in the sky with a New York skyline.

Theatrical Hotels

Because British actors usually stay in hotels if they go over to play on Broadway, some of them are listed here. There aren't any equivalent hotels in London, except perhaps for the Savoy and the Ritz where theatre people such as Charlie Chaplin, Orson Welles, Somerset Maugham, Noel Coward and Tallulah Bankhead stayed when in London.

The Algonquin

The Algonquin Hotel, on West 44th Street, has been the home to most of the British contingent of actors for over fifty years. What hotel in the world could boast of a guest-list like the Algonquin? — Noel Coward, Gertrude Lawrence, John Gielgud, Laurence Olivier, Charles Laughton, Bea Lillie, Jonathan Miller, Ian McKellen, Peter Ustinov, David Hare, the Redgraves, Jeremy Irons, Anthony Hopkins, Trevor Nunn, Tom Stoppard, Peter Hall, Angela Lansbury and Diana Rigg. A few of the Irish, like Lady Gregory and Brendan Behan, join Americans such as Orson Welles, the Barrymores, Douglas Fairbanks, Alfred Lunt, Lillian Gish and Burgess Meredith.

The American contingent was no less distinguished - Lillian Gish, Alfred Lunt, Helen Menken, all the Barrymores, Ina Claire, John Drew, Orson Welles (who spent a honeymoon here), Douglas Fairbanks (ditto; he also sold soap to the management before achieving stardom), Ruth Gordon, Dorothy Stickney, Burgess Meredith and Arthur Hunnnicut, who was an Algonquin dishwasher before gaining fame on Broadway and in Hollywood. Walter Huston got up one night in the Oak Room night-club and sang *September Song*, his show-stopper from *Knickbocker Holiday*. Recent visitors include Lily Tomlin, Gordon Davidson, Richard Dreyfuss, Jason Robards, Carroll O'Connor, Tommy Tune, Celeste Holm, Natasha Richardson, Bernadette Peters, Liza Minnelli and Kevin Kline.

Playwrights, no less than musicians and actors, found a home here. George S Kaufman (*The Man Who Came to Dinner*), Edna Ferber (*Dinner at Eight*), and her novel, *Show Boat*, are perhaps the best known. Lerner and Loewe wrote *My Fair Lady* and *Brigadoon* in Loewe's suite at the Algonquin.

The famous Round Table, or as they called themselves, "The Vicious Circle", consisted of nine regulars of whom the most remembered are Dorothy Parker, George Kaufman, Alexander Woolcott, George Jean Nathan, Robert E Sherwood (*The Petrified Forest*), Robert Benchley and Edna Ferber. The group started in 1919 with a lunch given to welcome Alexander Woolcott back to New York and *The New York Times*, on which he was the hated and feared drama critic. After the lunch someone said, "Why don't we do this every day?" and so they did, for ten years.

Apart from the regulars, others sat in from time to time. Noel Coward remarked to Edna Ferber, "You look almost like a man," to which she replied, "So do you." Robert Benchley was outside a New York hotel when it began to rain. He said to a uniformed and be-medalled man standing beside him, "My good man, could you get me a taxi?" only to receive the reply, "I'm not your good man, I'm an admiral in the US navy." To which Benchley immediately riposted, "Well then, get me a battleship."

The Algonquin has played a major role in the history of Broadway and continues to do so today. For years, they have hosted Playbill's monthly George Spelvin lunches, which feature casts of current Broadway shows.

Theatre awards' voting sessions are held annually behind closed doors. The Algonquin has hosted countless Broadway opening and closing nights. One of the great "closing night" parties was the one in 1933 that marked the end of Prohibition, with Marilyn Miller and Clifton Webb, stars of *As Thousands Cheer*, leading the revellers that thronged The Algonquin's lobby.

Near the conclusion of his 1977 book about the Round Table, *Wit's End*, James R Gaines writes, "None of them ever bid a genuine goodbye to the Round Table - one, that is to say, which neither excoriated it for its foolishness nor pretended that the group had been fabricated by the press for its own delight, the line to which Kaufman resorted in later years." Perhaps, as they avoided with humour the vulnerability of a fixed position, they were unwilling to identify themselves too much in public with a group whose stature in the thirties was undecided. Woolcott, the one with most to gain from the association and the one whose extremes of sentiment would be most likely to produce roseate hindsight, also deferred writing about the subject, except to say in a letter to John Peter Toohey shortly before he died, "I should enjoy seeing just once more those old chums that I still dislike with a waning intensity." Parker recalled, "... that not particularly brave little band that hid its nakedness of heart and mind under the out-of-date garment of a sense of humour."

Continuing the tradition today in the Oak Room cabaret, the imperishable songs of Broadway are performed and preserved for future generations. Each evening in the lobby Broadway music resonates. And in-house guests may view film versions of popular Broadway musicals via the closed-circuit TV system.

Years later, John F Kennedy said, "When I was growing up, I had three wishes - I wanted to be a Lindbergh-type hero, learn Chinese and become a member of the Algonquin Round Table."

The Plaza

The building of the present Plaza started in 1905, after the demolition of an earlier Plaza hotel on the same site. Construction took two years, the interior decoration and furniture was French, and it was intended to be the most luxurious hotel in the world.

At the beginning, it was used primarily as a town home for people who had houses elsewhere; the Vanderbilts were the first residents. Zelda and Scott Fitzgerald also lived there (Zelda is supposed to have danced naked in the fountain outside), and very many distinguished theatrical and artistic personalities were associated with it. George M Cohan held court in the Oak Room; Enrico Caruso was so infuriated by the humming of an electric clock that he is said to have destroyed it with a knife. Mrs Patrick Campbell stayed there on her first visit to the United States for her performances in *Hedda Gabler*. She smoked a cigarette in the Palm Court, causing a minor scandal. The Beatles stayed there for six days in 1964; Frank Lloyd Wright stayed for six years during the construction of the Guggenheim Museum, which he designed.

It changed hands many times; Donald Trump and Conrad Hilton were among the better known owners. It last sold for three hundred and twenty-five million dollars in 1995.

The Plaza has been used as a locale for countless films. Some of the most noteworthy were: *Barefoot in the Park, Funny Girl, Plaza Suite, Arthur, Crocodile Dundee*, and *Sleepless in Seattle*. The hotel publicity suggests that it has featured in more than three hundred films.

Truman Capote threw the 1966 Black and White Ball in the Grand Ballroom. Guests included Frank Sinatra and Mia Farrow (then just married), Vivien Leigh, Lauren Bacall, Steven Sondheim and Andy Warhol.

The Oyster Bar, opened at the end of 1969, was patterned after an English pub, and with its Edwardian-era murals quickly became a favourite of New Yorkers.

The Waldorf Astoria

No visit to New York would be complete without a stop to see the Waldorf Astoria hotel at 301 Park Avenue. Here is one of the all-time great theatrical hotels where the legendary Cole Porter lived - his piano is still played in the main lobby - as well as dozens of famous stars. The Duke and Duchess of Windsor lived for a time in the Waldorf Towers. So much has been noted in actors' biographies, it is difficult to name one or two, without leaving out your favourite star. When unemployed and down, you can always feel the past sitting in Peacock Alley sipping a martini. Most everyone did it at some time or another. Often celebrities meet for a drink there and at any given time you might have met Ginger Rogers, Fred Astaire, Gene Kelly, Noel Coward or Ivor Novello.

A word here about Cole Porter - and his lifestyle. The lyrics of Cole Porter remind us of the glamorous style he and his contemporaries lived in when they were in New York. If he wasn't travelling to Europe, staying in Venice, he was at the Waldorf Astoria.

When Noel Coward was asked to list things that had style he included any Cole Porter song. Coward understood as a playwright how written words should be performed. Elsa Maxwell, the famous party giver was a close friend of Porter and he wrote one of his best songs for her birthday, *I'm dining with Elsa*.

He wrote he was dining with Elsa and her ninety-nine most intimate friends. She gave parties in Paris, Venice, London and, of course, New York. She said her job was to entertain the rich. When the Waldorf Astoria first opened, they offered her a free apartment in return for establishing the hotel as "the" place to be. They also gave Cole Porter his penthouse at a small fee for the same reason. People like Elsa and Cole formed the elite society circle which centred around them. She knew everyone. She was never boring and most of her guests found her entertaining.

The city of Venice had hired her to promote the Lido and so she and Cole Porter and his millionaire wife went there for the summer in 1923.

When Cole returned to New York he put the district of Harlem on the map. During the thirties and forties Harlem was where white folks, the Cafe Society, went to hear jazz. The Cotton Club became famous and it was the place to go after the theatre.

Cole Porter and his wife, Linda were Broadway celebrities after his success with *Anything Goes*. Their lifestyle was written up in all the papers. Cole's songs had everyone dancing to his music. Hollywood wanted him, but Cole stayed home at the Waldorf to write. Later on he met Moss Hart, the playwright. They went on a world cruise with their wives and he took his own piano. They were known as "Miss Linda and her gentlemen". It was on this cruise they wrote the show *Jubilee,* and Cole composed *Begin the Beguine*. Finally he did go to Hollywood. Sophisticated New Yorkers, including Dorothy Parker considered the place a joke, even though she also wrote for the films.

Hollywood loved Cole Porter and he was a great success, but Linda did not and she left him to return to New York.

When the story of his life was filmed, (*Night and Day*) Cary Grant played the role; it omitted that he was a homosexual, although married to an extremely wealthy woman, and played down his wealth and lifestyle. He had become a living legend. They invited guests such as CBS chairman, William Paley, playwright, Robert Sherwood, and Charlie Chaplin to their lavish dinners. He went to see Coward's play *Quadrille* with the Lunts.

My parents came to visit me from Australia for Dad's eightieth birthday in 1980. I wanted to take him to the Waldorf to celebrate, but it was one of the hottest days on record so I tried to flag down only air-conditioned taxis - no mean feat in Manhattan. Either there are dozens of cabs around, or absolutely none at all. In the rain they are as scarce as hens' teeth. Mid-afternoon, the heat finally got to Dad, he said he was feeling very faint. I'd got tickets for the theatre that night, so what to do? You could feel the

35 *Above* The Oyster Bar at the Plaza Hotel, entrance on 58th Street.
36 *Below left* Murals decorate the Oyster Bar.
37 *Below right* Alec Guinness, Maggie Smith and many British stars prefer Wyndhams on West 58th Street, opposite the Plaza Hotel. The location is close to Broadway.

38 *Above* Afternoon tea at the Plaza Hotel.
39 *Below* Old King Cole Room, St Regis Hotel.

40 *Left Eloise at the Plaza*; famous book written by Kay Thompson, close friend of Noel Coward.
41 *Above right* Approaching Times Square.

42 *Right* Irish Repertory Theatre - some of the fringe theatre in New York includes the Irish Repertory Theatre on West 22nd Street. Frank McCourt's play and other Irish playwrights are featured here.

43 *Above left* Cafe des Artistes - originally a small hotel where many British theatre people stayed, including Noel Coward. Near the Met at the Lincoln Center, it is a favourite of Placido Domingo, James Levine and many opera stars. Address: One West 67th Street.
44 *Above right* The famous murals by the painter Howard Chandler Christy.
45 *Left* The lobby of the Chelsea Hotel is an art gallery.

46 *Above* Cole Porter's piano in the Waldorf Astoria.
47 *Bottom left* Hotel Chelsea's front door is surrounded by plaques in memory of the writers and artists who lived there, including Dylan Thomas and Brendan Behan.
48 *Bottom right* A famous rendezvous - under the clock in the lobby of the Waldorf Astoria.

49 *Above left* William Shakespeare - British writers in New York's Central Park.
50 *Above right* Robert Burns - British writers in Central Park.
51 *Below left* Tavern on the Green, a favourite restaurant of British performers in Central Park.
52 *Below right* Walter Scott - British writers in Poets' Walk in Central Park.

53 *Above left* The garden in Central Park is dedicated to John Lennon - it's across the street from the Dakota apartments where he lived.
54 *Above right* A mosaic in Strawberry Fields in memory of John Lennon.
55 *Below* The front entrance of the Dakota on Central Park West where John Lennon was killed.

56 & 57 *Above* The St Regis and Delmonico's - these hotels feature in British actors'
biographies.
58 *Below* Theatre Circle - a favourite place for books and gifts.

heat and humidity coming up from the pavements as you walked. It was well over ninety degrees. I flagged down a cab to the Waldorf. The cool air greeted us in Peacock Alley, and after a cool drink things began to look better. By 6 p.m. he was hungry. I went to the maitre d' in the dining room, but as Dad wasn't wearing a tie, he said we couldn't enter. I informed the maitre d' that Dad was a hugely rich Australian sheep-farmer who didn't need to wear a tie anywhere - maybe it helped and suddenly he gave us a table behind a pillar. The rest of the evening went well except for having to share a cab in the rain to the theatre.

Suggestion: Eat near the theatre. Don't count on getting a taxi between 6 and 7.30 p.m. anywhere in Manhattan if it's raining.

The Hotel Chelsea

The Hotel Chelsea, 222 West 23rd Street, between 7th and 8th Avenues, first opened in the 1880s when 23rd Street was the heart of the theatre district. Sarah Bernhardt stayed here and also Vladimir Nabokov. It is now a decaying Edwardian building which has obviously seen better days. Dylan Thomas spent his last days there, and Bob Dylan wrote a song about it. Some Britishers may remember Edie Sidgwick, the close companion of Andy Warhol, who lived in a studio apartment here. The film, *The Chelsea Girls*, was made here. The whole area around the hotel makes an interesting daytime walk and further south at 17 West 16th Street is the home of Margaret Sanger, one of the pioneers of birth control. Her house is now painted purple with a Greek-pillared front doorway, which for fifty years was the headquarters of her Clinical Research Bureau.

Other Hotels

Wyndhams on West 58th Street is a favourite of Alec Guiness and is a very low-key hotel compared to the glossy Plaza opposite - lovely interior decorated rooms.

The Edison Hotel, built in 1936, on completion had the lights switched on by remote control by Mr Edison himself from his home in New Jersey. The Art Deco designs in the lobby still stand, and it is worth a visit to see the kind of place that featured in the early movies and was the home of many British thespians in those times working in New York.

Chapter Ten

Three Walks Through New York's Theatreland

Walk One

Starting at West 44th Street just west of Broadway, you will find Sardi's restaurant on your left with the Helen Hayes Theatre next door. Helen Hayes was often named the First Lady of the American Theater. She was a stage star for over fifty years, retiring in 1971. With a long list of leading roles, she had a great success playing *Mary of Scotland* (1933) and *Victoria Regina* (1935). Lynn Redgrave starred in her own show, *Shakespeare for my Father*, at this theatre. Opposite is the Shubert Theatre next to Shubert Alley. The history of the Shubert Organisation, their theatres, would fill one book alone, but it is interesting to stand outside the entrance knowing you are in the heart of Theatreland. The Shubert brothers are legendary; the Shubert organisation currently manages its sixteen theatres on Broadway. The heartbeat of the firm is upstairs in offices over this theatre. Walk further down the street to see the St James's Theatre on your left. It opened in 1927 with a George M Cohan musical. It was here that *Oklahoma* (five-year run), *The King and I* - starring Gertie Lawrence in her last stage appearance - had long runs. Originally named the Erlanger Theatre it has 1600 seats. Highlights of the 1960s included Laurence Olivier in *Beckett*, Albert Finney in *Luther*. More recent productions include Jim Dale in *Barnum* and Twiggy in *My One and Only*. Cross the street to the celebrated Majestic Theatre. It was here that *Camelot* opened in 1960 with Richard Burton and Julie Andrews, and in 1988, *Phantom of the Opera*. Because of its large seating capacity, musicals have been frequently moved here when they become hits, such as *42nd Street*.

Walk up Broadway to 45th Street, then turn right to find the Lyceum Theatre. If possible try to see the historic penthouse apartment of the theatre which is the home of the Shubert Archive, but once was the apartment of Daniel Frohman, the original owner/producer. He lived there with his wife, the actress Margaret Illington, and the peephole in the apartment which was made so he could watch her performances is still there. It is the oldest Broadway theatre still in operation, and was declared a landmark in 1975. Two British plays which were hits in the 1960s were *A Taste of Honey* by Shelagh Delaney which starred Angela Lansbury and

Joan Plowright (who won a Tony award), and Harold Pinter's *The Caretaker*, starring Alan Bates, Robert Shaw and Donald Pleasance. Later came John Osborne's *Look Back in Anger*.

Across the street is the original Stanford White building which used to house the famous Lambs Club, but is now a church (see Theatre Clubs).

Cross Broadway to see the Booth Theatre at 222 West 45th Street which completes the western wall of Shubert Alley - which originated as a fire passage behind the legendary Hotel Astor, now gone.

Too many theatres' histories together tend to become a blur - but each theatre on this street has a list of British stars who have played here. Theatre histories are included in every theatre's programme - which, by the way are free of charge in New York.

Across the street to the Music Box Theatre to see the plaque in the lobby in honour of Irving Berlin (see photo). The Music Box was named by Irving Berlin, and he was half-owner with the Shubert Organisation until his death. His musical, *Of Thee I Sing*, became the first musical to win the Pulitzer Prize. Further on, is the Martin Beck Theatre at 302 West 45th Street, where the Irish Abbey Players and the D'Oyly Carte Company played. The 1,300 seat theatre was named after a leading vaudeville producer of the 1920s. Also on West 45th Street is the Plymouth Theatre, built in 1917 by Arthur Hopkins as a theatrical home for himself and his productions. The Royal Shakespeare Company's production of *Nicholas Nickleby* ran for eight hours with a dinner intermission and tickets were $100, a record price in 1981. Leslie Howard played Hamlet here in 1936.

As you cross Times Square you can see the statue of Mr Broadway, George M Cohan, on the pedestrian island in the middle of the street. As a rest from looking at theatres, walk down Restaurant Row on West 46th Street between 7th and 9th Avenues. Joe Allen's is on the left, Don't Tell Mama on your right, and a dozen other theatre restaurants that will offer you a pre-theatre dinner. Joe Allen's is the most famous with theatre people. Don't Tell Mama has a cabaret room where showcases are held for new talent as well as regular shows with well-known performers. Many songwriters try out material here with the favourite performers singing their works. The latest cabaret room to open in the area is The Firebird on West 45th Street. Cabaret is more popular in New York as an entertainment, than in London, it seems, with many more rooms to hear musical revues and performers.

Walk back along West 47th Street from 8th Avenue towards Broadway, the Brooks Atkinson Theatre is on your right, named after the eminent drama critic of the *New York Times*. Tallulah Bankhead made her final appearance here. In 1990 Nigel Hawthorne won a New York Tony Award for his performance in *Shadowlands*, the British play about C S Lewis. In the 1980s Rex Harrison, Claudette Colbert and Lynn Redgrave starred in Frederic Lonsdale's play, *Aren't We All?* British actors who have played here are Albert Finney, Zena Walker, Tom Courtenay and Paul Rogers, among many others.

Across the street is the Ethel Barrymore Theatre. This beautiful theatre was built by the Shuberts in honour of the beloved Ethel Barrymore and opened on 20th December 1928 with the actress starring in *The Kingdom of God*.

In the 1930s Fred Astaire made his last Broadway appearance here in Cole Porter's *Gay Divorce*, Katharine Cornell and Laurence Olivier in *No Time for Comedy* and it is where Maggie Smith, Michael Redgrave, and Michael Crawford have played. Orson Welles' production of *Moby Dick* with Rod Steiger was first presented here.

Walk up Broadway to West 55th Street, turn left to the Hotel Edison to relax in the Art Deco lobby.

Walk Two

Start at West 72nd Street subway station, cross Broadway and walk to Central Park along 72nd Street. On your right, you will pass the Triad Theatre. This is similar to the King's Head Theatre in Islington, London, in that they both produce plays and revues regularly but on a limited budget. You sit at tables and can order food, liquor or soft drinks before the show. It is one of the most reasonable ticket prices in town.

Further on, at the corner of Central Park West, stands the Dakota apartment building, the former home of Leonard Bernstein and many theatre celebrities. John Lennon was killed outside the front door, but his widow Yoko Ono still lives there. Cross the street into Central Park and follow the path to Strawberry Fields. This garden is dedicated to the memory of John Lennon. Notice the plaque inlaid with mosaics in memory of his song, *Imagine*. The garden is maintained by a grant from Yoko Ono. Turn right and walk up West Drive past the lake, turn right onto the path on the north side of the Belvedere Castle. Between the cottage and the castle is the Shakespeare Garden, where many of the plants there are mentioned in Shakespeare's plays.

Walk back to Broadway, and see the famous Ansonia Hotel at 2109 Broadway. It is one of the most celebrated apartment houses which was rescued at the last minute from the demolition crew. Since the turn of the century, the Ansonia has been a home for the arts in New York

City. No other building in the city has - for such a period of time - acted as a centre for the performing and creative arts, most notably, music and opera.

Originally built in 1904 to be the most elegant residential hotel in the nation, the Ansonia was quickly adopted by musicians, singers, writers, artists, teachers and coaches as a place to live and work. Because of its ornate beaux arts style, the building acquired this nickname: "The Wedding Cake" of the West Side.

There is more substance to that phrase than meets the eye, because the Ansonia truly represents a unique marriage of architecture and utility: the suites in the building, many of them circular or oval, are soundproof. Their acoustics are superb. High ceilings are "insulated" by a special construction system from the floors above. Interior walls are solid stone. A unique method of air circulation, which made the building the first "air-conditioned" structure in New York, still keeps interior temperatures at comfortable levels even during hot summers.

Today, the building is more important as an arts centre than at any period in its history, because of its nearness to the Lincoln Center, America's cultural complex.

Note the plaque over the front door. Caruso, Teresa Stratas, Toscanini, Theodore Dreiser, Sol Hurok, Lily Pons, Igor Stravinsky and Florenz Ziegfeld are among the former residents. Opera stars still reside there, as it is so close to the Opera House. The lobby has been renovated, but the desk man told me that it used to be much larger, a huge elegant space with magnificent chandeliers and a pool with live fish and a fountain.

Walk down Broadway to 71st Street, turn right along 71st Street to 211 West to find, on your right-hand side, Applause Theatre Books. This is a great theatre shop where you can find dozens of play scripts, film scripts, show business books of all kinds, videos - it is a "must" for all theatre buffs.

Continue down Broadway to the Lincoln Center. Here you will find the Metropolitan Opera House, the City Opera and the Avery Fisher Concert Hall. Go inside the entrance of the Opera House to see the murals by Chagall. If you are there in the summer, you might catch an outdoor concert in Damrosch Park, just by the side on the left of the Opera House. There are two theatres on the opposite side, where the New York producers try out new plays and smaller productions, the Mitzi E Newhouse and the Vivian Beaumont.

Cross the street to West 67th Street and perhaps end your walk with a drink at the Cafe des Artistes on the left-hand side just before you reach Central Park West. (See chapter on Theatre Restaurants)

Walk Three

Besides the actual theatres of Broadway, there are many dramatic and colourful venues in New York which attracted the British performers when staying in New York. Their New York counterparts would entertain them, wine and dine them in the glamorous hotels and restaurants in Manhattan. Their friends were writers, painters, musicians as well as theatre people, people such as Scott Fitzgerald, Dorothy Parker, Kay Thompson, Neysa McMein, the Lunts. On this walk you will visit some of these places which are still as popular today as they were fifty years ago.

Start at the Plaza Hotel on Fifth Avenue at 59th Street. Walk through the main lobby to see the renowned Palm Court. It is located amid a profusion of greenery in the heart of the Plaza Hotel's lobby, long recognised as one of the premier meeting places in New York and an enchanting European café at the hub of the Plaza lifestyle. Filled with serenades of piano at lunch and piano and violin from afternoon tea until late evening, the Palm Court is a lively indoor cafe that hums with activity from early breakfast to après-theatre dining. It is reminiscent of an outdoor English cafe where people-watching is a beloved pastime.

This was the same Tea Court sacred to the memory of the elegant Edwardians, later the popular haunt of the thirties as the Palm Court, and still later, the luncheon setting for calorie-conscious ladies who nibbled on salads; the place where, as *New York Times* society editor Russell Edward wrote, "Nobody raises an eyebrow if you order tea at cocktail time."

A 1907 guest would be just as at home in today's Palm Court, which the builders then called The Lounge and guests called The Tea Room. It was modelled on the lines of the wonderful Winter Garden in London's Hotel Carlton, but with special touches all of its own. The domed ceiling was executed in pastel green and yellow leaded glass for the hotel by Louis Comfort Tiffany, but was removed in 1944 as part of Hilton's renovations. The French-style mirrored rear wall has accented arches supported by four marble caryatids, representing the four seasons. Columns and table-tops were made of fleur de pèche marble, and today, sixty to sixty-five tables are said to be original.

A few days after the hotel opened on 1st October 1907, they looked down upon young Gladys Vanderbilt, who lived in her father's house across the street, sitting in the Tea Room with Count Laslo Szechenyi, saying yes to his offer of marriage. It was the beginning of still another tradition, courting at The Plaza.

The British actress, Mrs Patrick Campbell, arrived at The Plaza from England on 8th November 1907 for the theatrical engagement, *Hedda Gabler*.

Travelling with her seventeen-year-old, and blind, monkey-spitz poodle, one week later, on 15th November, she lights a cigarette in the Palm Court, making herself the first woman in America to smoke a cigarette in a public place. Her response to management was, "My dear fellow, I have been given to understand this is a free country. I intend to do nothing to alter its status."

One result of her folly was that smoking was banned on subways two years later.

Over the years, a lot of less-than-romantic people have tried to change the Tea Room into something different. But, fortunately for romance, the room isn't much different today from what it was in the beginning. The Tiffany ceiling is gone, unfortunately, victim to the removal of the open courtyard above it, and the name has been changed. They began calling it the Palm Court in the mid-1930s.

Turn left to see the portrait of *Eloise* on the wall in the hall. Kay Thompson, a close friend of Noel Coward, wrote a series of books about this fictional and mischievous six-year-old. The book is still sold in the hotel's Gift Shop and continues to be a best seller. *Eloise* became a favourite with the French too, when it came out in Paris.

Kay used to stay with Coward at his homes in England and Switzerland; they used to play two-piano duets together, and she was always included when he entertained. Kay was a gifted singer, writer, arranger, made her Broadway debut in 1937, and also had a successful cabaret act which was performed at London's Cafe de Paris. Her one-woman show ran on Broadway in 1954.

On the other side of the Palm Court is the Oak Room, where a plaque to George M Cohan (Mr Broadway) can be seen in the far right-hand corner above the booth where he always sat, plotting Broadway shows and doing business. He wrote the famous song, *Give my Regards to Broadway* (see the chapter, The Great White Way). Don't miss the Edwardian elegance of the murals in the Oyster Bar.

F Scott Fitzgerald and his wife Zelda were, for a time, residents. They loved the hotel. Ernest Hemingway once advised Fitzgerald to donate his liver to Princeton and give his heart to the Plaza.

Cross Fifth Avenue and go south to West 55th Street, turn left to the St Regis Hotel. This is where the Oliviers stayed. The mural in the King Cole Room was painted by Maxwell Parrish, and used to be on the wall in Rector's, the celebrated restaurant on Broadway, before it closed many years ago. Take the elevator up to the roof to view the lovely ballroom. The most lavish balls and parties were held here for the Windsors, and after first nights. They still are! Ivor Novello, Noel Coward all partied here.

Continuing along West 55th Street to Park Avenue, turn south to the Waldorf Hotel at 50th Street. It is here, in the Waldorf Towers, that the Windsors lived when they were in New York, in the residential part of the hotel. Cole Porter lived there too for over twenty-five years. His piano used to be in Peacock Alley, off the main lobby, but it has now been moved to the Terrace Room above the foyer. Pianists still play it for afternoon teas and the cocktail hour. Somerset Maugham, Winston Churchill, Elizabeth Taylor have all stayed at the hotel, and it is still full of the atmosphere of that gilded jazz age of the 1920s.

Walk across along 49th Street back towards Fifth Avenue and you will come to the famed Rockefeller Center. Walk through the building, to see the Art Deco sculptures on the walls both inside and outside, the outdoor skating rink, and then take the express elevator up to the top of the building to see the view from Rainbow Room. (see Theatre Restaurants).

Back down again, exit on Sixth Avenue, and walk down 45th Street, one block west across to Times Square, to the Half Price ticket booth perhaps, for tickets for that evening's show; if you can face another elevator, go across to the Marriott Hotel on Times Square and take one of their glass elevators up to the revolving bar and restaurant, which overlook theatreland and Times Square, for a drink or dinner.

In New York people don't go to the theatre - they go to see hits.

Louis Jordan

CHAPTER ELEVEN

FRINGE THEATRES OF NEW YORK - OFF BROADWAY

Broadway was the birthplace of the American musical. In the pre-war world of the jazz age, glamour, glitter and stars, there were dozens of theatres on Broadway.

Then came Off Broadway in the 1950s. They are smaller theatres with a hundred to two hundred and ninety-nine seats, using Equity actors on contract.

Off Broadway producers have the courage to present plays by unknown playwrights, often without-name-players, and many of them are subsequently transferred to Broadway.

Here are the names of some of the most well-known ones, but there are many more, although some of them don't stay open on a year-round basis. Always check the newspaper or *Time Out* for the current programmes.

Circle in the Square is New York's oldest company, founded in 1951. Theodore Mann produced many of O'Neill's plays. Jim Dale worked there in 1974 in *Scapino*, Rex Harrison in *Heartbreak House* in 1983, and Tom Courtney in *Uncle Vanya* in 1995. Many of the productions transferred to Broadway, and numerous awards include Tonys, Obies and Drama Desk Awards. Off Broadway theatres first produced plays such as Beckett's *Endgame*, Joe Orton's *What the Butler Saw, The Elephant Man*, C Churchill's *Cloud Nine* and Bennett's *A Chorus Line*.

The Manhattan Theatre Club on West 55th Street started in 1970 to develop new work. Lynne Meadow, the Artistic Director since 1972, says that their aim is to present well-crafted, challenging plays by major writers from the US and around the world. Known as the MTC to New Yorkers, Lynne received the 1989 Drama Desk Award for setting such high standards at MTC and encouraging new playwrights as well as importing plays from abroad.

Joseph Papp (1921-1991) was founder of the New York Shakespeare Festival in 1954. He began his career as a stage manager on Broadway, but then in 1966 obtained a huge hundred-year-old building at 425 Lafayette Street, on New York's lower East side, and there began the Shakespeare Theatre Workshop. There are five theatre spaces within the building, and in 1992 the huge complex was named after Papp in honour of the late producer whose influence in the theatre will long be remembered.

Playwrights Horizon was founded in 1971 to develop new plays and produce them. André Bishop, the artistic director from 1981 to 1991, worked with a stable of resident playwrights who included Christopher Durang, A R Gurney and Wendy Wasserstein. The new plays included *The Dining Room*, *The Heidi Chronicles*, and *Driving Miss Daisy*. They also hold readings and work shops.

The two theatres at the Lincoln Center are the Mitzi E Newhouse and the Vivian Beaumont. The Vivian Beaumont is a part repertory theatre which was planned by Elia Kazan and Robert Whitehead. The theatre opened in 1955 and attracted many of New York's top directors and managers. Among them came Gregory Mosher, from Chicago's Goodman Theatre, and Bernard Gersten, a Broadway producer. Then came André Bishop from Playwrights Horizon who appointed Nicholas Hynter as an associate director. Joseph Papp also was involved with the company before his death. There are always new plays and readings taking place there.

One of the most celebrated theatres is the Lucille Lortel Theatre on Christopher Street, named after one of the most well-known women in New York theatre. She began producing plays in 1941 in her barn in Westport Connecticut, and it became a great showcase for new plays during the summer season. She re-modelled it and called it The White Barn Theatre. In 1955 she acquired the Theatre de Lys in New York, and it was renamed the Lortel in 1981. It served as a transfer theatre for the more successful plays at the White Barn. Carol Churchill's *Cloud Nine* was first produced here following plays by Brecht, Genet, Fugard and Ionesco. Her first production in New York was *The Threepenny Opera*, which ran for seven years. She is a co-founder of the American Shakespeare Festival, and a documentary film was made about her, called *The Queen of Off Broadway*.

Off Broadway theatre actors have included Kevin Kline (*Hamlet*), Geraldine Fitzgerald (*Mass Appeal*), George C. Scott (*Present Laughter* and *Design for Living*), also Julie Harris, Claire Bloom, Meryl Streep, Stacy Keach and Jason Robards Jr. Off Broadway is a place for well-known actors to try unfamiliar roles. In 1955 the *Village Voice* newspaper established the Obie Awards to reward productions Off Broadway, and there are also the Lucille Lortel awards given each year.

Finally, the new location for the show, *Forbidden Broadway*, is worth noting as it is now on West 51st Street on Broadway. This show is a revue, well worth a visit if you enjoy watching American actors lampooning British shows as well as all the current Broadway hits. Wicked impersonations of Julie Andrews, Andrew Lloyd Webber, Natasha

Richardson are all part of the game. This revue updates its material each season to parody the current Broadway shows. Created by Gerard Alessandrini, who is a genius in writing new lyrics to Broadway songs, it has been running since 1982. After Madonna had made her Broadway debut, Alessandrini changed the song in *My Fair Lady - The Rain in Spain stays mainly in the plain* -to *We tried in vain to train Madonna's brain*. For years the location was Off-Off Broadway, but now the location is more in line with its name.

Off Off Broadway

Off Off Broadway became established in the early 1960s. There are now around two hundred theatre spaces in Manhattan, from tiny theatre stages in old churches, lofts, cafes and sometimes store fronts; these productions can range from traditional three act plays to one man shows. Again it is necessary to check each theatre's programmes on a weekly basis, as many of them have short runs, or a repertory system with different plays on alternate evenings.

In 1975 when Robert Mosher, who was the director of Playwright Horizons, needed a theatre, he discovered a group of buildings on West 42nd Street which were being used as massage parlours, porno shops etc.: he rented one space and he ended up by completely transforming the area. He successfully obtained an alternative theatre district a few blocks west of Broadway for Off Off Broadway companies.

The 42nd Street Redevelopment Corporation was formed, and they bought the whole block of buildings. In 1978, with much publicity, Theatre Row was officially opened. There were ten companies, all operating on a non-profit basis, and some of these companies have since been upgraded to Off Broadway status.

Restaurants and small cafes opened, and there is subsidised housing complex for actors called the Manhattan Plaza nearby. Theatre Row now houses the following theatres: the Acting Company, Alice's Fourth Floor, Theatre Arielle, the Samuel Beckett, the Harold Clurman, the Douglas Fairbanks, the George S Kaufman, INTAR Hispanic American Arts Center, the John Houseman Center, the Judith Anderson, the Nat Horne Musical Theatre, Playwrights Horizons (main stage and studio theatres), and the Theatre Row Theatre. Many British actors have performed there including Fiona Shaw in T S Eliot's *The Wasteland*.

A word must be recorded here about the Theatre Guild, which was formed in 1915 by a group of young actors and writers who were dissatisfied with the commercial theatre of their day.

They organised a company called The Washington Square Players - way off Broadway - and they were ambitious enough to try to become a professional company, eventually to present plays on Broadway. The Guild's record is unique in the history in the history of the American Theatre, and it is only recently that it has ceased production.

Cafe Cino was the first Off Off Broadway theatre, where Joe Cino presented plays in his coffee-house in 1959. Cafe La Ma Ma was founded by Ellen Stewart in 1962, and Theatre Genesis by Ralph Cook in 1964. New playwrights were discovered including Sam Shepard, Terence McNally and Lanford Wilson.

We live in what is, but find a thousand ways not to face it.
Great theatre strengthens our faculty to face it.

Thornton Wilder

Chapter Twelve

My Own Journey to New York

When I arrived in New York, I did not have cocktails at the Rainbow Room, nor check into the Plaza, nor stay at the Algonquin. I did not hear Benny Goodman's jazz, the only music at night was the noise of garbage trucks and sirens. I had a small room in a playwright's house in exchange for typing up play scripts and sorting out her files.

My first job on Broadway was not on stage, but backstage, working as Yul Brynner's personal assistant during his final run of *The King and I*. After he died, I took a job as a receptionist behind the Red Door at Elizabeth Arden's Salon on Fifth Avenue. I was in charge of booking appointments for facials and make-up sessions. At the beginning it was a novelty. My curiosity was aroused by facing the women who came in. Some were successful professionals, stylish business women but most were wealthy housewives. Within a very short time I quit in exchange for sitting alone at the dining room table in my apartment trying to finish writing my play, and rationalising the lost income. The apartment had very little light, almost like a cave, but it was quiet so no excuse not to get on with it. I had sent out my first play several months earlier to agents, theatre managers and producers. There were piles of rejection slips and no progress at all.

I sent the script out to several Off-Off Broadway producers, they all came back. In desperation I attended sessions at the New Playwrights, The Actors' Studio and several theatre sessions, all to no avail. I began walking the streets, knocking on doors of small theatres to try to get the personal attention of producers and directors.

When I first went to New York I came across a small theatre, Off Broadway - a few blocks from Broadway named The British Theatre Company. I went to one of their shows and afterwards spoke with the producer/director of the company. As in the London fringe theatres, the professional actors, sometimes very well-known names, work for nothing or for car expenses only. I was used to this fact in London and expecting her to mention this but one of her questions surprised me. She asked how many friends did I have? I misunderstood her for a minute or two - it was not the usual question like what have you done, or where is your bio? I wondered suddenly if personal and social attributes were more important than talent. She repeated the question with still no interest in my résumé! As I was a newcomer to Manhattan I certainly didn't know many people, let alone friends. She then explained. If I could guarantee fifteen people at each performance (to pay half the rent) then she might hire me. She had no subsidy.

I thought this was incredibly crass at the time, but since becoming a producer myself I now know exactly what she meant. On a grander scale, it is the old "star" system, the pulling power at the box-office. You must have a "following" she said, and I couldn't in all honesty say that I did! As a producer, you have to pay the rent, and even if your actors are brilliant, if they don't help publicise the show, or are well-known, you play to empty houses. Full stop! Advertising in newspapers was astronomical.

Finally I found a theatre and producer. We had three weeks' rehearsal time. As it was my first experience as a director, and since it was not in some provincial town, I was nervous, apprehensive, but also very excited. Towards the end of the second week, I went with the producer to a large warehouse full of new furniture. He asked me to pick out the pieces I wanted for the set. The set designer had already started the actual set, but he wanted me to choose what I liked. The set was a smart beach-house outside Sydney, with white bleached floors and a large patio. The pale beige sofa and carpets fitted in well.

In the meantime, every day when not at rehearsals, I was dashing around trying to promote, publicise and sell the play. Letters and press releases had to go to producers, newspapers, organisations, libraries, other fringe theatres and clubs. Off-Off Broadway theatres do not have the budget to publicise each production so it is up to the cast, playwright, director and everyone involved with the play to do as much as they could.

At the beginning of the third week, I came home after rehearsals and there was a message on my machine from home in Hobart, Tasmania. It was from my father's doctor. I called him immediately. Dad had just had a heart attack, and things looked bad. He asked if I was free to fly out to Australia, as he might not recover.

Anyone who has suddenly had a phone call from home at a critical time in their lives knows the feeling of shock and confusion. I spent a sleepless night trying to decide what to do. No decision could be made until the next day. If I flew home I would miss the opening and obviously the one-week run as well.

In the morning I phoned home again. Dad had survived the night and was in a stable condition. The worst was over. I explained my circumstances to the doctor, and he said to ring back the next day. So walking back to the theatre that morning, my head was dizzy with indecision. It was difficult to concentrate, as we started the first technical run-through, but the play was just about ready to open. A write-up in the *New York Times* was uplifting, especially as all the other press releases seemed to have fallen on barren ground.

That evening, another phone call to Australia gave me a reassuring talk with the doctor. Dad was much better, there were no further complications, and after a week or so in hospital, the doctor felt that Dad would be back home. He suggested I delay my flight for the time being. The care he was getting from Mum and the hospital staff would be fine. So the crisis was over, even though it was stressful and worrying, to say the least. Why is it that one can work so hard at a project, then something happens to nullify it all. The theatrical profession seems more vulnerable than any other. The lyrics of *There's no business like show business* say it all.

Saying to the doctor, "I have a play opening in a few days' time" sounded so trivial. God, what egotism, how uncaring! The play might go on but my father might be dead. Which had the priority, your father or your play? Fortunately I didn't have to make that choice.

The show opened without any major disaster, and went well with one or two good reviews. It didn't transfer to a larger house, but I was satisfied that it was well done. There are so many fringe theatres in New York, so many productions, that it would be impossible to see them all - especially for main-stream producers. Friends advised me to hire a PR person to publicise the show, but at $15,000 a throw, I couldn't afford it.

My third play, *To Kill a Critic*, was about the murder of a well-known New York theatre critic and again the casting was difficult. However, we started rehearsals and all was going well until the lead actor was offered a highly-paid television commercial - so off he went. I then came up with the idea of double-casting the play, and as we had four weeks run, the first cast would do the first two weeks and the second cast do the third or fourth weeks. I would then have two of every character and if one had to drop out we would have a replacement. Rehearsals were divided and I did not allow each cast to watch the other. Often as a director, there was the opportunity to create stage business for one character entirely differently from the second cast. In actual fact, it was a good plan because the mother in the show at the last minute had to play in both casts as the second mother developed health problems.

One of my main concerns was security in the theatre. The building also housed several court-rooms operated by the Police Station next door - so there were always strange characters lurking in the corridors and staircases. The dressing-rooms were off the foyer of the theatre, nowhere near backstage, so, if we were all in the theatre rehearsing on stage, all our clothes were a fair distance away. I can remember trying to locate a locksmith to replace the broken lock on the night of the dress rehearsal. While actresses were parading on stage asking for my decision on a sudden change of costume, the lighting man changing the lights on a whim, the stage manager announced that the front door or phone "bell" didn't work or that a prop had disappeared, asking for changes at the same time while a myriad of tiny requests and details came at me from all sides; but my main concern was to be able to sit in the theatre in peace directing the show without us all being robbed of our possessions in the meantime. As most of the cast, if not on stage would be in the wings waiting to go on, I knew there was a very real risk. To keep this worry from the actors was hard going - they had their lines to worry over, so I sat at the back of the auditorium with one eye on the foyer watching the locksmith.

Fortunately there were no quick changes of wardrobe and the cast were relieved to be told of the new arrangements after the show. However, as we were leaving the theatre, I realised that someone had nicked in and taken my address book from the table at the back of the theatre. What use is your address book to someone else, I wondered? It took weeks to adjust to the loss of it.

Producing fringe theatre can be exciting and rewarding particularly if you help someone to move up dramatically in their career. The camaraderie is the same as in professional theatre, maybe more so because these performers often have to work at other jobs to be able to do fringe. My last leading man was an auxiliary relief fireman - emergency staff. A handsome talented actor, I was always alarmed that he might be called away. I wouldn't allow myself to imagine him up a ladder, fighting a fire in Hell's Kitchen which was just down the road. Fortunately the occasion never arose. Many weeks of trying to help actors and write special material for them individually was rewarding as I know how hard it is to get someone to help initiate things. The stakes are very high for these actors who often lose their day jobs because of their dedication to attending rehearsals. They are involved in a very personal and financial way.

After we had finally resolved the problem of the dressing-room lock, things settled down as much as they could on a dress rehearsal. There was a ladder up to the lighting-box and each evening I would watch the rather elderly, but fiercely loyal, lighting-man negotiate the gap between the top of the ladder and the platform of the lighting rig. Dozens of trivial problems occurred that might cause actors' minor complaints - forgotten props, missing stage manager. (He'd gone out for more props or his take-away dinner at the same time as wailing police sirens came up the street to the police station.) The tension was building to the first night. Under the circumstances it was all rather fraught. Why do we do it? Kenneth Branagh, in his extraordinarily touching film, *In the Bleak Mid-Winter*, wrote a heart-rending speech which every actor could identify with. His group of actors were having even worse problems putting on *Hamlet* in a freezingly cold church in the north of England. The director suddenly and violently explodes with emotion: "What is the point? What is the fucking point? It is too personal for us all. What is the point in going on with this miserable tormented life? I mean can anyone tell me, please, please, what makes this fucking life worth living?"

How brilliantly Branagh put it!

Walking home after the first night, which went well, I was loaded down with the more valuable props that I didn't want to leave in the theatre. Halfway through the night I got up to get a glass of water, and suddenly missed my purse with keys, money etc. in it. Oh my God, what next? - surely I must have had it when I came in as I needed the key to open the door. After frantically searching around without success, I opened the apartment's front door and there was my bag on the floor in the corridor, by the door where I had put it down to carry in the props. It was still there, and this was New York! Obviously no one had passed my door since I had arrived home. One less thing to worry about. It is always the little things one remembers when the big things are crowding in.

Many theatre people talk about tenacity. I admire writers who can keep writing plays even if they are never produced. Somerset Maugham wrote plays for ten years before one was produced, remarkable perseverance. Even though he did have the subjects and plots to hand, the work is grindingly hard.

To avoid the day-time distractions, I began to get up at 4.30 a.m. to write. They say the brain is fresh at that time, the flow of words easier. I wonder. It seems unnatural to be writing when everyone else is asleep. A poet friend of mine can write verse travelling in a car, sitting in a restaurant, or, indeed, anywhere when the Muses strike - better than staring at a white piece of paper at 4.30 a.m., I thought.

The Fringe theatre, in New York as in London, presents dozens of new plays, but very seldom do we hear of a huge success with transfer to Broadway or the West End; nevertheless good work is done and this training ground for actors who may or may not keep another career is still invigorating.

My father recovered, and lived on for six months.

Why is it that we must write when the odds are so great? The combination of wanting to act, to direct, to write is always present, but if you can't make a living out of it, the frustration becomes so great that even the strongest need some kind of financial return or encouragement.

The walk home always helped relieve the stress. When would we get a break? Walking up 6th Avenue I walked straight into Peter Hall. He was four feet away. With a shock of recognition I said, as he was passing, "Sir Peter?" He smiled and nodded and then was gone. Why hadn't I stopped him and asked him to come to see my play? The moment was lost. There goes the best break that we'd ever get.

Those kind of surprises do happen in New York. Another example: my son Colman came face to face with Phil Collins in Central Park - however they did stop and talk for a minute or so, as Colman is a big fan of his, and he didn't let the opportunity escape as I had done.

Quoting Branagh again, "It's not about fame or money or so-called wealth and security; it's about nourishing your soul, nourishing your heart."

Fame is the spur. But money is the problem.

In my book, *From Shakespeare to Coward*, I wrote about the escape from winter weather in England and even though the theatre was the motivating force for working in Britain, the icy winds and depressing climate drove me to search for warmer climes. Part of life in the theatre is to study characters, plots, drama from everyday life. Stimulation, energy coupled with curiosity comes with the trade. New experiences are essential to keep actors, directors and all theatre people motivated. So it was the same when living in North America. However, the winter is even more severe. Although you don't have the same endless weeks of drizzling rain and grey skies as in England, you do have weather which is below zero temperature with bone-chilling cold. During one particularly cold winter, I escaped to Nassau in the Bahamas and fell in love with the place. Descending from the plane, walking across the tarmac and inhaling the hot, humid perfumed air is one of those few acute pleasures which is never forgotten. The softness of the air after the cold is glorious. The palm trees, vivid flowers and greenery hit you like a thunderbolt, and immediately the whole world changes. You drop twenty years. I quickly found out why so many British people had made their winter homes there. Whereas some well-known Brits had escaped to the south of France, such as Somerset Maugham and Graham Greene, many had gone to the Bahamas.

In the first week I met the actor, Richard Harris, who had a house on Paradise Island, and next door was Kevin McClory who co-produced the James Bond films. Those two certainly knew how to live, with floodlit pools, Jacuzzis, outdoor feasts and the ever-present rum punches.

It was at his house around his pool that I met the wonderful Irish actress, Shiobhan McKenna. I knew I had to stay the winter ... but how to survive? It was obvious I'd have to find a job. Everyday there were stories of illegal employees being thrown off the island with twenty-four hours notice only. Work permits were almost impossible to obtain. I had a bet with a yacht owner for $5000 who bet that I would not be able to obtain a permit, let alone a job. I proved him wrong, and when challenged, he quickly set sail overnight, disappearing to one of the other seven hundred islands in the sun, or probably to Florida.

The only way I managed to obtain a work permit and a job was because a Canadian tour company needed a bilingual representative to communicate with the many French-Canadians holidaying on the Islands. I brushed up my French and gave new arrivals briefings on what to do and what to see in Nassau.

It was an acting job of sorts, after all, I rationalised. You really had to act to cheer people up, if, after they had saved up for a year to spend a week in the sun, it rained for the entire time, which it sometimes did. Cheerfulness was all. Then people would start to complain that the pictures on the wall in their room were crooked, or that they couldn't stand the wallpaper.

I quickly organised entertainment for them, and tried to make them forget the weather. During our training we were told what to do in many circumstances, from someone dying overnight in their room to being mugged and robbed outside a night-club, not necessarily in that order. But during my first week on the job, most of the guests went down with food poisoning from the "Arrival Dinner", something not covered in my training. Another time the hotel had double-booked all the rooms, so when my group of forty people showed up on Christmas Eve there were no rooms for them. You had to deal with alcoholics, women becoming hysterical on losing a child, or the ones who had just left their husbands at home, à la Shirley Valentine, and with whingers, amateur deep-sea fishermen falling overboard, jellyfish bites, and compulsive gamblers. One phone call came at six a.m. from a chap who had gambled away everything, and didn't have enough money to pay for a taxi to get to the airport. Would I please drive him? Could I also lend him a few dollars to get home from the airport?

Life stories were poured out as the rum punches flowed.

People who had suffered a recent bereavement always came at Christmas which was the worst time for grieving. I would sit and listen to their accounts of their dear departed always made much worse by the loneliness of a hotel room in the company of strangers.

It certainly increased my exposure to the human race as well as experiencing first-hand some incidents that normally don't happen back home.

It was surprising how much history there was to discover, and, besides sitting on the beach or playing golf, there were some interesting tours. In the evening there were the usual native shows and casino spectaculars, but also some talented artists who would come to the hotel to perform. One legendary singer, a local Bahamian, was Wendel Stuart. He was an exceptional talent, a cross between Harry Belafonte and Sammy Davis Junior. He would bring his guitar and sing calypso and local songs as well as singing for the children in the audience. He won the Musician of the Year Award in Nassau many times and wanted to go to New York to try to break into the big time as Belafonte had done.

Many fans would fly in from the mainland to hear him and one fan with his private jet would fly in from South Carolina every weekend to catch his show.

Even though the Bahamas gained their independence from Britain in the 1970s there was still a great deal of the British influence there. The old British Colonial Hotel, downtown at the end of Bay Street still held the charm of colonial days. Government House, nearby upon the hill, used to be the home of the Duke and Duchess of Windsor, and, of course, Lyford Cay still is the home of many celebrated British writers and theatre people. Much of this old world charm has gone with the huge development of giant tourist hotels, but in some areas it still remains.

The first season I was there, a Canadian group of actors were producing plays in the hotel ballroom, and several one-man shows were brought out from England. One of the first James Bond movies, *Dr No*, was shot in Nassau, and many movie companies followed including The Beatles in their film, *Help*. The company I worked for, SkyLark Holidays, also decided to make a promotional film there, which was a fun experience. Julian Prins, who wrote the script, was the Director of Sales and Marketing for SkyLark, and he made the film for distribution to hundreds of travel agents promoting a holiday in the Bahamas; in three days we filmed what most tourists would take ten days to cover. Julian has now gone on to worldwide recognition as one of the top marketing directors in the industry although he could have followed with equal success his other passion, to become a symphony orchestra conductor. Wendel Stuart's music was featured in the film, and it was great to go and hear him play in Greenwich Village when he and his wife finally got to New York.

Back in North America again, still with no acting work but warmer weather than in London, I worked for a television show called *The Palace*.

It was a musical variety show backed by a forty-four piece orchestra on stage and guest host, Jack Jones. It was a weekly show and each week we would have two or three celebrity guests introduced by Jack. During the run of the show we had people such as Jerry Lewis, Ginger Rogers, Ethel Merman, Charles Aznavour, Michel Le Grand, Tina Turner and Rolf Harris, and, when Pearl Bailey and Lou Rawls were scheduled, I managed to book Wendel Stuart as well. He stole the show and was brought back on stage several times. Tragically he died of leukaemia a few years later, and was taken back to Nassau to be buried in "the land of the sea and the sun", the title of the song he sang so well.

Today I still travel, lecturing on the QE 2, which is theatre in a way, only you don't get blinded by the footlights.

POSTSCRIPT

PLAN YOUR OWN SHOWCASE

For performers or producers who would like to present a showcase in New York, the most affordable venues, of course, are Off-Off Broadway. Some of the locations are very central and not far from Broadway. The most expensive are the small theatres along Theatre Row on 42nd Street, but there are other spaces available which you can rent for one performance, one week or one month, depending on you budget. The Producers' Club is a good venue for a showcase.

New Yorkers are keen on British performers and new plays, so if you advertise your show in *Time Out* and the *Village Voice* you should get an audience. The American Theatre of Actors has three theatres, and if Jim Jennings, the artistic director, is not producing a play, he rents the theatres out.

There are several other theatre companies in that area, and it is essential to pick up a copy of the trade paper, *Backstage*, to find them. *Backstage* has casting and audition notices also, for Equity and non-Equity work. Professional companies usually cast through a casting agency, so that is the best way to proceed. The fringe theatre is easier to break into in New York, because there are so many spaces, and producers looking for new plays and performers.

USEFUL ADDRESSES

1	Algonquin Hotel - 59 West 44th Street
2	Applause Theatre Book shop - 211 West 71st Street
3	Cafe des Artistes - 1 West 61st Street
4	Chelsea Hotel - West 36th Street
5	Dakota Apartments - West 72nd Street. Strawberry Fields at West 72nd Street in Central Park
6	Delmonico's - Park Avenue at East 62nd Street
7	Players Club - 16 Gramercy Park
8	Plaza Hotel - 59th Street at 5th Avenue
9	Sardi's - West 44th Street
10	Theatre Row - between 9th and 10th Avenue on West 42nd Street
11	Triad Theatre - West 72nd Street
12	The King Cole Room, St. Regis Hotel, West 55th Street
13	Open-air Theatre, Central Park at 78th Street Great Lawn
14	Half-price Ticket Booth, Times Square

Off Broadway Theatre

American Place Theatre - 111 West 46th Street between 6th Avenue and Broadway

Forbidden Broadway - Stardust Theatre, 1650 Broadway at West 51st Street

Irish Repertory Theatre - 132 West 22nd Street between 8th and 9th Avenues

John Houseman Studio Theatre - Theatre Row, West 42nd Street

Joseph Papp Public Theatre - 425 Lafayette Street between 4th and 8th Streets

Manhattan Theatre Club - 131 West 55th Street between 6th and 7th Avenues

Minetta Lane Theatre - 18 Minetta Lane off Sixth Avenue

Promenade Theatre - 2162 Broadway at West 76th Street

Roundabout Theatre - 1530 Broadway at West 45th Street